A-LEVEL YEAR 2

STUDENT GUIDE

AQA

Business

Topics 1.9 and 1.10

Strategic methods: how to pursue strategies

Managing strategic change

Mike Pickerden

HODDER
EDUCATION
AN HACHETTE UK COMPANY

Hodder Education, an Hachette UK company, Blenheim Court, George Street, Banbury, Oxfordshire OX16 5BH

Orders

Bookpoint Ltd, 130 Park Drive, Milton Park, Abingdon, Oxfordshire OX14 4SB

tel: 01235 827827

fax: 01235 400401

email: education@bookpoint.co.uk

Lines are open 9.00 a.m.–5.00 p.m., Monday to Saturday, with a 24-hour message answering service. You can also order through the Hodder Education website: www.hoddereducation.co.uk

ISBN 978-1-4718-5691-4

First printed 2017

Impression number 5 4 3 2 1

Year 2021 2020 2019 2018 2017

This Guide has been written specifically to support students preparing for the AQA A-level Business examinations. The content has been neither approved nor endorsed by AQA and remains the sole responsibility of the author.

Typeset by Integra Software Services Pvt. Ltd., Pondicherry, India

Printed in Italy

Cover photo: Giuseppe Porzani/Fotolia

Hachette UK's policy is to use papers that are natural, renewable and recyclable products and made from wood grown in sustainable forests. The logging and manufacturing processes are expected to conform to the environmental regulations of the country of origin.

Contents

■Getting the most from this book

Exam tips

Advice on key points in the text to help you learn and recall content, avoid pitfalls, and polish your exam technique in order to boost your grade.

Knowledge check

Rapid-fire questions throughout the Content Guidance section to check your understanding.

Knowledge check answers

1 Turn to the back of the book for the Knowledge check answers.

Summaries

■ Each core topic is rounded off by a bullet-list summary for quick-check reference of what you need to know.

Exam-style questions

Commentary on the questions

Tips on what you need to do to gain full marks, indicated by the icon ⓔ

Sample student answers

Practise the questions, then look at the student answers that follow.

Commentary on sample student answers

Read the comments (preceded by the icon ⓔ) showing how many marks each answer would be awarded in the exam and exactly where marks are gained or lost.

Questions & Answers

(a) Analyse how the Co-operative Bank could use Lewin's force field analysis to manage change in the way it runs its business. [9 marks]

ⓔ 'Analyse' questions expect you to develop a line of argument. It is not necessary to make several points; usually two points (at most) that are well explained and use the case study would be sufficient.

(b) Analyse how a strategy of retrenchment could improve the profitability of the Co-operative Bank. [9 marks]

ⓔ In this question you would be expected to show good understanding of retrenchment and to explain fully at most two ways that it could improve the Co-operative Bank's profitability. Each argument should be illustrated with examples from the case study.

(c) Do you think that changes in the external environment have been the main cause of the Co-operative Bank's poor business performance? Justify your view. [16 marks]

ⓔ The phrase 'Do you think...' is often used in exam questions. It invites you to consider one argument for the proposed reason and one argument against, before making a justified conclusion that definitively states whether you agree or disagree.

Student A

(a) Lewin's force field analysis is a useful technique managers can employ when trying to manage change. Lewin said that the first step was to identify where there is a need for change. In the case of the Co-operative Bank, this could be the mis-selling of PPI. The next stage would be to identify all the reasons for the change and all the factors against it. For example, a reason for the need to change the mis-selling of PPI is the financial penalties that the bank will suffer if it continues. A reason against the change could be staff resistance, as perhaps they received bonus payments for each PPI policy sold. Lewin then said that each reason for and against change should be given a score and then an overall total. If the total for change was greater, then it should be implemented. In the case of the need to stop selling PPI, it is obvious that the score for change would be higher because of the severe financial consequences to the Co-op Bank if it doesn't do this.

Another benefit of Lewin's theory is that it identifies which reasons either for or against change are the most important. If there is significant resistance from staff about changing the way PPI is sold, the senior managers could then focus on how to reduce this resistance. For example, they could introduce a different payment system for staff who sell PPI. By doing this, change can be implemented more smoothly.

ⓔ 9/9 marks awarded. A very good answer that reveals excellent understanding of Lewin's theory. Two separate reasons are identified and well developed with consistent use of the case study.

74 AQA Business

■ About this book

This guide (Student Guide 4), along with its companion (Student Guide 3), has been written with one aim in mind: to provide you with the ideal resource for your revision of the second year of the AQA Business A-level. The topics covered in this guide build on the knowledge gained during the first year of the course.

In your study of the subject you will look at business in a variety of contexts: small and large, national and global, service and manufacturing.

The overall focus of the second year of the AQA Business A-level is analysing the strategic position of a business, choosing strategic direction, assessing strategic methods and managing strategic change. The study of strategic decision making builds on the study of decision making in the functional areas in the first year of the course.

Central to this specification are the following themes:
■ The impact of technology on strategic decision making.
■ The influences of Corporate Social Responsibility, and ethical and environmental issues, on strategic decisions.
■ The difficulties in forecasting future trends.
■ The importance of assessing feasibility and risk when making strategic decisions.
■ The impact on stakeholders of strategic decisions and their response to such decisions.

The focus of Book 4 is the following:
■ Strategic methods: how to pursue strategies.
■ Managing strategic change.

The Content Guidance section offers concise coverage combining an overview of key terms and concepts with identification of opportunities for you to illustrate the higher-level skills of analysis and evaluation. Read through the topic area before attempting a question from the Questions & Answers section.

The Questions & Answers section provides examples of the various types of questions that you are likely to be faced with: multiple choice, short-answer, data-response, case study and essay questions.

A common problem for students and teachers is a lack of resources, in particular of exam-style questions that cover individual areas of study. The questions in this guide are tailored so you can apply your learning while the topic is still fresh in your mind, either during the course itself or when you have revised a topic in preparation for the examination. Along with the sample answers, this should provide you with a sound basis for sitting your exams in Business.

Content Guidance

■ Strategic methods: how to pursue strategies

Assessing a change in scale

The reasons why businesses grow or retrench

The reasons why businesses **grow** include:

- **To increase profitability** – by increasing market share in existing markets or targeting new markets, a business would expect to increase its sales revenue and profitability.
- **To become more efficient** – increased demand leads to increased production. Increased production should lead to higher levels of capacity utilisation. As a result, fixed costs are spread over more units of production, resulting in lower unit (average) costs. In the long run, as a business expands it should benefit from economies of scale, which lead to lower unit costs.

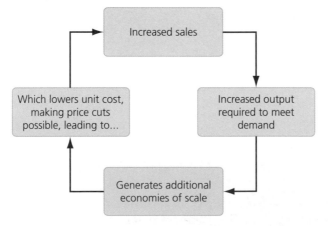

Figure 1 How increased sales lead to lower unit costs

- **To gain market dominance** – through growth a business can increase its market share and become the market leader. The business can also increase its range of products, which can be aimed at different market segments. By gaining market dominance, the business can make demand for its products more price-inelastic, as consumers develop brand loyalty and/or have fewer alternative products to choose from. This enables the business to charge higher prices and as a result to benefit from increased revenue and larger profit margins.
- **To achieve managerial objectives** – by achieving increased growth, the directors of a business will often be rewarded with bonuses and share options. This provides them with a financial incentive to achieve higher levels of

Business growth is when a business expands through opening more factories and/or retail outlets. Growth can occur both domestically and internationally. It is often a measure of business success.

Knowledge check 1

Explain how business growth should lead to increased profitability.

profitability through growth. Furthermore, the directors may also be motivated by the psychological benefits of achieving successful growth, such as increased recognition and status.

The reasons why businesses **retrench** include:

- **To survive a recession** – demand falls as a result of reduced consumer spending during a recession. This means that a business may have to cut production, resulting in lower levels of capacity utilisation. Lower levels of capacity utilisation cause higher unit costs, as fixed costs are spread over fewer units. In order to survive, a business may decide to reduce its capacity and fixed costs by closing down an under-utilised factory.
- **To improve competitiveness through delayering** – a business can reduce its staffing costs by removing layers of management. It may also speed up decision making because information must pass through fewer levels of hierarchy. This should make a business more responsive to changes in its market. For example, it may be able to respond to changes in consumer trends more quickly and exploit this by bringing out new products faster than the competition.
- **To prevent losses at the end of a product's life cycle** – during the decline phase the sales of a product fall below its breakeven point. As the product is no longer profitable and may be using up valuable resources, a business may decide no longer to produce it.
- **To strategically change direction** – a business may decide to close down divisions and/or stop making loss-making products, and instead to focus on its 'core' products, which generate the greatest proportion of sales and profits. By selling off under-performing divisions, a business can then raise the cash needed to invest in its more profitable operations.

Exam tip

You may be asked questions requiring you to evaluate the main reason why a business decided to grow or retrench. Remember to consider both the strengths and weaknesses of the particular reason you have chosen in comparison with the other reasons.

The difference between organic and external growth

Organic growth occurs when a business expands from within. This can be achieved in a manufacturing business by increasing capacity from opening new factories. In service sector businesses, growth is achieved by opening more retail outlets.

External growth results from a takeover or merger with another business. A takeover occurs when one business acquires more than 50% of the other business's shares. A merger occurs when the owners/shareholders of two businesses agree to bring them together.

How to manage and overcome the problems of growth or retrenchment

During a period of retrenchment, the biggest problem is the effect on morale. Retrenchment usually involves redundancies. In addition to the cost of redundancies,

Retrenchment is the opposite of growth. It is the process by which a business slims down its operations. This will usually involve reducing capacity by closing factories and/or stores.

Knowledge check 2

Identify two reasons why Tesco has decided to go through a process of retrenchment in recent years.

Knowledge check 3

Explain why a takeover is often considered to be hostile, while mergers are usually friendly.

the business will also have workers who are unhappy at losing some of their colleagues, as well as suffering feelings of uncertainty regarding their own job security. This fall in morale can lead to industrial action and to poor productivity and quality.

To reduce these problems, it is important that a business fully consults with trade unions and offers voluntary redundancies first.

One of the most common issues resulting from internal growth is **overtrading**. When businesses expand, a significant cash outflow results from increasing factory capacity or from opening more retail outlets. The time required to construct these buildings and to install the necessary equipment means there is often a time lag between this cash outflow and the cash inflows that occur only once the factories and/or outlets are operational. During this time lag the business may run out of cash and could possibly become insolvent.

To avoid overtrading, a business must plan its cash flow carefully and ensure that it has access to additional funds to pay all its bills during this time.

Economies of scale are a benefit that a business hopes to gain from growth. There are three main economies of scale:

- **Technical economies of scale** result from investment in new technology such as capital intensive production, e.g. the use of robots in car manufacture. This method of production is more efficient, reduces wastage and improves quality, all of which result in a fall in unit costs.
- **Purchasing economies of scale** result from the bulk-buying discounts that larger businesses can obtain from suppliers, due to the increased size of their orders for raw materials and components. Large orders are attractive to suppliers, therefore the supplier has a big incentive to offer discounts.
- **Managerial economies of scale** result from the advantages larger firms gain from employing managers with specialist skills, e.g. accountants and lawyers. This should result in better decision making and reduce the chances of making expensive mistakes.

Economies of scope is another benefit of business growth. For example, Coca-Cola can manufacture a large range of different drinks more efficiently than a smaller specialist manufacturer that produces just one drink. This is because Coca-Cola has larger capacity and has the technology to enable it to switch production from one drink to another more flexibly.

While a larger business can enjoy the benefits of economies of scale, a key issue that may result from increased size is that of **diseconomies of scale**. There are three main types of diseconomy of scale:

- **Poor employee motivation** as a result of less contact with management. This can lead to feelings of alienation and lack of recognition from management. Poor motivation may result in increased absenteeism and falling labour productivity.
- **Poor communication** is often a problem in larger organisations. Organisational structures become more complicated, with increased levels of hierarchy. This often means that messages take longer to reach the intended receiver, resulting in slower decision making. Furthermore, communication often becomes more impersonal, for example occurring via email rather than face to face. This increases employees' feelings of alienation.

Overtrading is when a business suffers from cash flow problems as a result of expanding too quickly.

Economies of scale are factors that cause average (unit) costs to fall as the scale of output increases in the long run.

Knowledge check 4

Explain one benefit that a business can gain from lower unit costs.

Economies of scope lead to a fall in unit costs as a result of one business producing two or more separate items, compared to each item being produced by a separate business.

Diseconomies of scale result in an increase in unit costs due to a business becoming too big.

■ **Poor managerial co-ordination** occurs as larger businesses are more difficult to manage. Different functional areas may not communicate effectively with each other and senior managers may become unaware of potential problems. This can lead to falling efficiency.

Knowledge check 5

Explain why higher absenteeism and falling labour productivity could lead to higher unit costs.

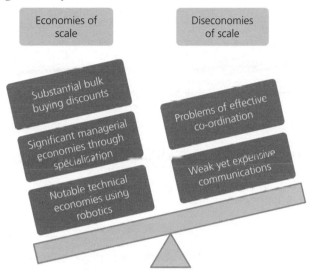

Figure 2 Economies verses diseconomies of scale

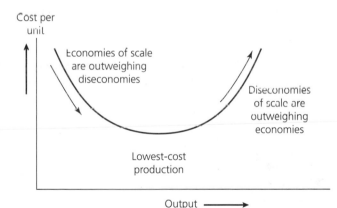

Figure 3 Production costs and production scale

Exam tip

The case study in AQA Paper 3 is usually based on a large business. When reading the case study, try and identify the potential economies and diseconomies of scale that the business could encounter.

The **experience curve** is another benefit gained from increased business growth. This theory considers that large businesses can enjoy sustained periods of market dominance over their smaller rivals due to their greater economies of scale. Larger firms also learn from experience how to produce more efficiently. Many firms, however, may be unable to maintain this dominance due to diseconomies of scale; companies such as Nokia and Tesco are good examples of this.

The **experience curve** shows the reduction in average costs that occurs when increased total output allows producers to learn from experience how to produce more efficiently.

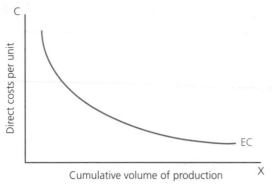

Figure 4 The experience curve

Synergy is another term often used when discussing the benefits of growth. When two businesses merge, for example, cost savings can result from needing only one head office or one finance department. Furthermore, increased revenues can result from being able to operate in more than one market.

Greiner's model of growth

In **Greiner's model of growth**, the six stages of growth are:
- growth through creativity
- growth through direction
- growth through delegation
- growth through co-ordination and monitoring
- growth through collaboration
- growth through extra-organisational solutions.

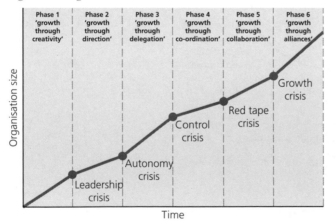

Figure 5 Greiner's model of growth

Source: adapted from 'Evolution and Revolution as Organizations Grow' by Larry E. Greiner, in *Harvard Business Review*, May 1998

Exam tip

Greiner's model of growth is a new theory in the AQA specification, and examiners may be keen to test your understanding of it.

Synergy occurs as a result of the increased revenues and/or reduced costs that occur as a result of two businesses becoming one from a merger or takeover. It means that the whole is greater than the sum of the parts.

Greiner's model of growth states that businesses pass through six stages of growth when they expand. Each phase begins with a period of stable growth, which is then followed by a crisis. When one of these crisis events occurs, the business must re-organise if it is to continue to grow and progress on to the next phase. Businesses that cannot make the necessary changes will get stuck and find it difficult to grow.

The impact of growth or retrenchment on the functional areas of a business

Each functional area will need to adapt its strategy in response to either growth or retrenchment. Table 1 illustrates some examples of the tactical decisions each functional area may have to make.

Table 1 The impact of growth and retrenchment on the functional areas of a business

Functional area	Impacts of growth	Impacts of retrenchment
Marketing	To expand, firms operating in competitive markets might have to emphasise better value for money in the marketing mix.	A firm retrenching might opt to scale down its operations by reducing its product range, or by exiting from specific markets. Budgets for promotion and new product development might be reduced.
Finance	Price cuts used to increase market share will reduce profit margins. Over-rapid expansion can also cause cash flow problems.	Redundancy payments could cause additional cash outflows in the short run. In the longer term, however, a smaller workforce should reduce the break-even output level by lowering fixed costs.
Human resources	Additional staff will probably have to be hired to cope with the extra workload.	Redundancy programmes can cause morale to decline among the workers who survive the job cuts. Some of the company's more talented members of staff might decide to leave before the next round of redundancies.
Operations	Production methods might have to be adapted to ensure that the additional demand created by the marketing department can be supplied.	Investment in new machinery and equipment is likely to be halted. Poor staff morale is also likely to cause productivity to fall, making the firm less efficient.

Assessing methods and types of growth

Methods of growth

Internal or organic growth occurs as a result of a business gradually increasing its sales and capacity. External growth occurs when a business expands by joining up with or acquiring another business. The main methods include mergers, takeovers, joint ventures and franchising.

A merger occurs when two businesses, usually of similar size, agree to join together. Ownership of the business is split equally between the shareholders of the merged companies. A takeover occurs when one business takes control of another business by buying at least 51% of its shares. Takeovers can be either hostile or friendly. Reasons for mergers and takeovers include:

- **Growth** – the new business is significantly bigger in terms of sales and capacity.
- **Cost synergies** – resulting from economies of scale.
- **Diversification** – reducing risk by selling in more than one market.
- **Market power** – increased market share compared to rivals.

Table 2 Reasons for takeovers and some examples

Reasons for takeovers	Examples
Growth	Facebook paid $19 billion for mobile-messenger WhatsApp in 2014 Kraft's takeover of Cadbury in 2010
Cost synergies	In May 2014 Carphone Warehouse and Dixons agreed to merge, saying they would enjoy annual cost savings of £80 million within three years Co-op took over Somerfield (it bid £1.7 billion in 2008); the result was a disaster
Diversification	Tesco bought 49% of Harris & Hoole coffee shops in 2013 Kellogg's bought Pringles crisps for $2.7 billion in 2012
Market power	Indian car producer Tata (producers of the world's cheapest new car) bought Jaguar Land Rover for £1.3 billion in 2008 Holcim's merger with fellow cement giant Lafarge gave the combined group a 50% market share in Canada, and not far short in Britain

Joint ventures occur when two businesses agree to work together on a specific project for a certain period of time. Usually ownership of the venture is split on a 50/50 basis. Often the businesses will join together to share their expertise in order to exploit a market opportunity. For example, many UK firms have established joint ventures with Chinese businesses in order to enter the Chinese market. The Chinese business provides valuable knowledge regarding consumer tastes, domestic competition and legislation. The UK business provides finance and expertise.

Franchising is when the owner of a business (the franchisor) allows individuals (the franchisees) to use his or her business model. In return, the franchisee pays the franchisor an initial fee plus a percentage of the sales revenue. The franchisor will also often provide training, store design and advertising. Well-known franchises include Subway, Specsavers and KFC.

Types of growth

Horizontal integration is when one business takes over or merges with another business in the same industry and at the same stage in the production process, e.g. Adidas buying Reebok. Horizontal integration is the most common type of external growth.

Vertical integration is when one business takes over or merges with another which is in the same industry but that operates at a different stage in the production process. Vertical integration can be either backward or forward.

Knowledge check 6

Identify two reasons why Google acquired YouTube in 2006.

Knowledge check 7

Identify two advantages to the franchisor of growing a business by selling franchises.

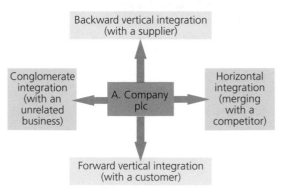

Figure 6 Vertical and horizontal integration

An example of backward vertical integration is when a manufacturer takes over a supplier, e.g. a car company acquiring a tyre manufacturer.

An example of forward vertical integration would be a manufacturer taking over a retailer, e.g. a clothing company acquiring a chain of fashion stores.

Table 3 The advantages and disadvantages of backward vertical integration and forward vertical integration

	Backward vertical integration	Forward vertical integration
Advantages to the company	Closer links with suppliers aid new product development and give more control over the quality and timing of supplies Absorbing the suppliers' profit margins may cut supply costs	Control of competition in own retail outlets; prominent display of own brands Firm put in direct contact with end users/consumers
Disadvantages to the company	Supplier division may become complacent if there is no need to compete for customers Costs might rise, therefore, and delivery and quality become slack	Consumers may resent the dominance of one firm's products in retail outlets, causing sales to decline Worries about image may obstruct the outlet, e.g. Levi stores rarely offer discounted prices
Advantages to the workforce	Secure customer for the suppliers may increase job security Larger scale of the combined organisation may lead to enhanced benefits such as pension or career opportunities	Increased control over the market may increase job security Designers can now influence not only how the products look, but also how they are displayed
Disadvantages to the workforce	Becoming part of a large firm may affect the sense of team morale built up at the supplier Job losses may result from attempts to cut out duplication of support roles such as in personnel and accounting	Staff in retail outlets may find themselves deskilled. Owner may dictate exactly what products to stock and how to display them. This would be demotivating
Advantages to the consumer	Better co-ordination between company and supplier may lead to more innovative new product ideas Ownership of the whole supply process may make the business more conscious of product and service quality	With luxury products, customers like to see perfect displays and be served by expert staff, e.g. at perfume counters in department stores Prices may fall if a large retail margin is absorbed by the supplier
Disadvantages to the consumer	The firm's control over one supplier may in fact reduce the variety of goods available Supplier complacency may lead to rising costs, passed on to customers as higher prices	Increased power within the market could lead to price rises If the outlet supplies only the parent company's products, consumer choice will be hit, as in brewery-owned clubs or pubs

Conglomerate integration occurs when one business takes over or merges with another business in a different industry. An example was the takeover of Gillette (a shaving products business) by Procter & Gamble (a manufacturer of household cleaning products). A common motive of conglomerate integration is to spread risk through diversification.

Exam tip

When assessing the risks and rewards of a takeover, a useful theoretical model to use is Ansoff's Matrix.

Knowledge check 8

Explain one reason why conglomerate integration could be considered the most risky type of external growth.

Summary

From reading this section you should be able to:
- understand the difference between internal and external growth
- identify three reasons why a business might want to grow
- define retrenchment
- identify three reasons why a business may decide to retrench
- understand the concept of economies of scale
- explain technical, purchasing and managerial economies of scale
- define diseconomies of scale
- understand Greiner's model of growth
- identify three methods of external growth
- explain the difference between vertical, horizontal and conglomerate integration.

Assessing innovation

The pressures for innovation

Innovation enables a business to maintain a competitive advantage. If it fails to constantly develop new products or processes it could be overtaken by its rivals.

The pressures for innovation result from competitors, because in a competitive market a business needs to differentiate itself from its rivals. Innovation can enable a business to bring out better products and/or improve efficiency, quality and customer service. Other pressures for innovation come from the market, in that customers increasingly expect businesses to provide new improved products and high levels of service. Shareholders also provide pressures for innovation: businesses are expected to grow, increase their profitability and provide high dividends. Innovation is often crucial in achieving these expectations.

One type of innovation is process innovation, which is concerned with designing improved methods for manufacturing products. A business that can develop a production process that is more efficient and produces better quality products than its rivals may enjoy a significant competitive advantage.

Another type of innovation is product innovation. This is concerned with developing a brand new product or successfully improving an existing one. Product innovation often results from a combination of scientific and consumer market research.

> **Innovation** means developing a brand new idea for a product or a new manufacturing process and making it a commercial success

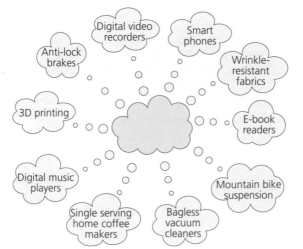

Figure 7 Examples of innovation

> **Knowledge check 9**
>
> What is the marketing term for introducing an innovative product on the market before the competition?

The value of innovation

The benefits from innovation for a business include:

- **Monopoly power** – by patenting an innovation, a business can protect it from being copied by its competitors. This means that customers can buy the product only from the actual business. This enables the business to recover its research and development costs quicker.
- **High prices** – because of its monopoly position, a business can adopt a price-skimming strategy. This enables it to enjoy high profit margins. These profits can then be reinvested into developing more new products and/or processes.
- **Improved reputation** – an innovative business will gain a good reputation, which will attract customers and consequently reduce the need to spend large amounts on marketing. The business will enjoy high levels of brand loyalty, because customers are always interested in businesses that consistently release new products.
- **Cost reduction** – process innovation results in a more efficient production system with less wastage and better quality. This enables a business to achieve higher levels of added value.

The ways of becoming an innovative organisation

Ways of becoming an **innovative organisation** are shown below.

Kaizen

This is a Japanese term meaning 'continuous improvement'. It is based on the principle that most ideas come from people rather than from technology and that change is incremental, based upon the cumulative effect of many small changes.

An **innovative organisation** is one that continually develops and implements new ideas that help it achieve its goals.

Figure 8 The kaizen culture

The culture of kaizen is based on:

- **One employee, two jobs** – as well as actually performing their job, the employee is also expected to think of ways to improve it.
- **Teamworking** – employees work in teams (or 'cells') and are expected to meet regularly to suggest and discuss ideas for improvement.
- **Empowerment** – employees are given the power to implement their ideas for improvement.

Research and development

Scientific and technical research can lead to both process and product innovation. It is particularly important in sectors such as pharmaceuticals, technology and engineering. Research and development spending costs, however, are often high and outcomes uncertain. UK businesses tend to spend less on research and development than their foreign competitors. In the long run this could have negative consequences for the international competitiveness of UK firms.

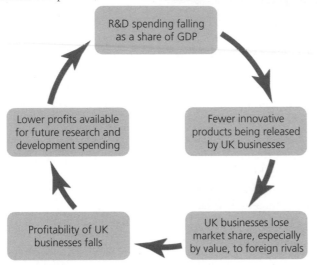

Figure 9 The importance of research and development (Source: OECD, March 2015)

Intrapreneurship

Intrapreneurship is when large businesses encourage their employees to act like entrepreneurs by coming up with new ideas, which they will then support with financial and other resources. For example, Google allows its employees to spend one day per week working on their individual ideas. Other businesses hold 'innovation days' or have staff competitions for coming up with the most innovative idea.

Benchmarking

Benchmarking is when a business finds out how the best companies achieve their outstanding performance and then tries to implement their ideas. Often these ideas come from businesses that operate in different industries and are willing to share them.

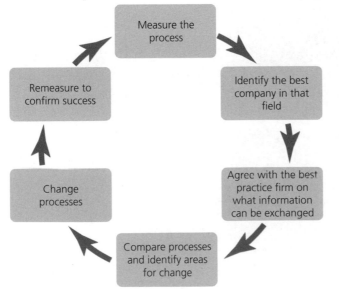

Figure 10 The benchmarking process

Knowledge check 10

Explain which motivational theorists can be linked to kaizen and intrapreneurship.

How to protect innovation and intellectual property

Intellectual property can be protected by patents or copyrights.

Patents

These provide the inventor with a period of twenty years during which his or her work cannot be copied by anyone else. In the UK, patents are issued by the Intellectual Property Office. The benefit of a patent is that it encourages innovation by giving businesses legal protection. Without patents, businesses would be discouraged from developing new products because their competitors would simply copy them. Applying for a patent can be expensive and time-consuming, however.

> Intellectual property is the general term for assets that have been created by human ingenuity or creativity. They can include music, literature and inventions.

[handwritten: barrier to entry]

Table 4 The impact of patent rights

	Impact on companies holding patents	Impact on competitors	Impact on customers
Positive	Gives monopoly power for up to 20 years Prices can be higher and competition subdued Creates incentives to develop new patentable opportunities	Makes it hard to enter the market competitively... ...which may force firms to be innovative in developing ways to get round the patent Some patents may prove too tough to get round	Fosters product innovation, which should benefit customers But prices can be higher due to monopoly power, e.g. drug treatments priced at more than £10,000 a year
Negative	Taking out patents is expensive, perhaps costing £75,000–£150,000 for global protection Strong patent rights may lead to complacency	May lead to unethical business practices such as industrial espionage	Ordinary people in developing countries cannot afford life-preserving, patented drugs

Copyrights

Copyright applies to written material such as books, newspaper articles, music and software. Copyright is similar to patents, as it prevents anyone else from copying the author's work. With the growth of the music, publishing and technology industries, copyrights have become increasingly important.

The impact of an innovation strategy on the functional areas of a business

Finance

An innovation strategy is likely to require significant long-term investment. For example, in the pharmaceutical sector research and development costs can amount to several million pounds and there is no guarantee that the research will lead to successful new drugs. The Finance department will need to use investment appraisal techniques in order to decide which projects offer the best return.

People

The majority of new ideas come from employees, so an innovation strategy will often involve employees from different specialist areas meeting regularly. Methods such as kaizen and intrapreneurship encourage a culture of team working and risk taking. The Human Resource department may have to organise training for employees so that they can learn how to use these techniques.

Operations

Innovative production processes often require the implementation of new equipment, machinery and materials. They may also involve employees having to learn new working practices. Implementing new processes often means overcoming 'teething problems' quickly to ensure that the efficiency and quality improvements are achieved.

Marketing

The development of innovative products is often key for a business to gain marketing advantages. For example, new products can use a price-skimming strategy, enabling the business to gain high profit margins. Also, distribution can be easier for innovative products because retailers are always keen to sell interesting new products. An innovation strategy will also require the marketing department to consider new ways of pricing, promoting and distributing products, however.

Knowledge check 11

Identify three ways that the growth of e-commerce has changed how businesses market their products.

Exam tip

Successful innovation is dependent on a range of factors. You may be asked questions that require you to consider which is the most important factor for a business that wishes to adopt an innovation strategy.

Summary

From reading this section you should be able to:
- define innovation
- explain the difference between process and product innovation
- identify three pressures on a business to be innovative
- define kaizen
- explain the costs and benefits of research and development spending

- understand the term 'intrapreneurship'
- define benchmarking
- explain the difference between a patent and a copyright
- understand how an innovation strategy impacts the functions of finance, people, operations and marketing.

Assessing internationalisation

Reasons for targeting, operating in and trading with international markets

One reason for **international trade** is profitability. By selling to overseas markets, a business has an opportunity to increase its revenue. This is because it increases its potential market by selling to countries with large populations. Furthermore, it may be able to reduce its costs by importing goods and services from a cheaper foreign supplier.

Growth is another reason for international trade. Selling overseas increases the potential market for a business, enabling it to expand. The business may also increase its capacity by opening offices, shops and factories abroad.

Selling internationally means a business can spread its risk by diversification. This is because it is not dependent on one market. So, for example, if the economy in the UK was in recession, the business could focus its sales on other countries that are experiencing growth.

International trade occurs either when a firm buys goods or services from another business operating abroad, or when it sells its products to an overseas buyer.

The different methods for entering international markets are:

- **Export** – a product is produced domestically but sold abroad.
- **Licensing** – a licence is a document that gives the holder the legal right to produce a patented product in exchange for a royalty payment. A UK business can give an overseas producer a licence to produce and sell its products. Coca-Cola will often give foreign soft drinks manufacturers a licence to make its products.
- **Alliances** – an alliance is a partnership between a UK and a foreign business. It enables the UK business to benefit from the foreign partner's knowledge and expertise in order to sell its products overseas. For example, Superdry established an alliance with a Chinese retailer in order to sell its clothes in China.
- **Direct investment** – this is when a business produces and sells its product abroad. For example, Jaguar Land Rover built a new factory near Shanghai in order to manufacture and sell its cars to the Chinese market.

> **Knowledge check 12**
>
> Can you think of three potential difficulties for a business that sells its products internationally?

Factors influencing the attractiveness of international markets

Market attractiveness is determined by market size and growth – countries with large populations are potentially attractive because of their market size. Furthermore, if the population is becoming wealthier, this creates opportunities for increased sales and profits. In recent years, China and India have become attractive to Western companies because of their huge populations and growing number of 'middle class' consumers who can afford Western products.

Market attractiveness is also determined by economic factors. Countries that are experiencing economic growth are attractive because rising levels of GDP indicate that consumers are becoming wealthier and have increased purchasing power. Emerging markets are particularly attractive to Western companies because their rates of economic growth are higher than those in Europe and the USA.

> **Market attractiveness** describes the likely profits that might be available to a business that is willing to enter a new market.

Table 5 The link between GDP and car purchasing for selected countries

	GDP per capita at PPP US$s (2014)	New car purchases (market size, 2014)	Population size (2014)	New car purchases per thousand people (2014)
USA	$53,000	16,400,000	318,892,103	51.43
UK	$37,500	2,476,435	63,742,977	38.85
Brazil	$12,100	2,504,161	202,656,788	12.36
India	$4,100	2,570,531	1,236,344,631	2.08

Other economic factors such as tax levels, inflation and unemployment also need to be considered as they will affect both consumer confidence and the amount of disposable income available to spend.

Other factors that influence market attractiveness include laws and regulations – countries that have strict laws regarding employment and consumer and environmental regulation may be less attractive due to the increased costs of operating there.

Political and social factors also affect market attractiveness. Some countries encourage foreign investment by offering grants and low taxation rates. Consumer trends also affect the attractiveness of a particular country. For example, in developing economies there is increasing demand for luxury Western brands such as Burberry and Gucci.

A final factor influencing market attractiveness is the quality of infrastructure. This includes facilities such as roads, railways, power, water and telecommunications. Countries with poor infrastructure are less attractive because this makes it more difficult for businesses to manufacture and distribute their products.

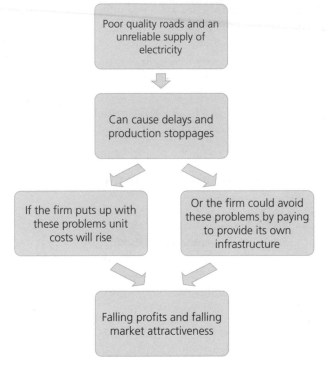

Figure 11 The impact of poor infrastructure on market attractiveness

Reasons for producing and sourcing more resources abroad

Many businesses have decided to **offshore** many of their operations overseas. The reasons for offshoring include:

- **Lower operating costs** – due to lower wages, rent, taxes and legislation, many Western businesses have moved their production facilities to developing countries. Lower operating costs enable these businesses to enjoy higher profit margins.
- **Distance** – to reduce transport costs, particularly for bulky items, it makes business sense to manufacture overseas. This also enables the producer to deliver products more quickly to its customers. For example, many soft drinks manufacturers have either built their own factories abroad or made licence agreements with domestic producers.
- **Trading blocs** – a trading bloc is a group of countries that allow free trade between them, but impose restrictions on imports and exports produced by countries outside the trading bloc. The European Union is an example. To avoid such restrictions, businesses from countries that do not belong to a trading bloc will open factories in countries within it. For example, many US corporations have opened factories in Eire in order to access the European Union.

Despite the benefits of offshoring, however, some businesses have decided to **re-shore** their operations back to their domestic country.

Offshoring is when a business transfers its production and other functions from its domestic country to one overseas.

Re-shoring is when a business decides to close its overseas operations and relocate them back to its domestic country.

Knowledge check 13

Give three reasons why a UK business may decide to re-shore its operations from China.

Ways of entering international markets and the value of different methods

Joint ventures

This is a partnership with a domestic business in which control and profits are split equally. The domestic business provides local knowledge and expertise, while the foreign business often provides direct investment and training of the local workforce.

Franchising

This is where a business sells franchises to entrepreneurs in overseas markets. As well as benefiting from the entrepreneurs' knowledge of customers' tastes, the franchisor is able to expand rapidly and with minimal cost. Examples of successful franchises include KFC, Subway and McDonald's.

Being a multinational business

This is when the business has its headquarters in its domestic country, but has operations such as factories, offices and shops worldwide. Examples of multinationals include Nike, Google, Starbucks and Ikea.

Influences on buying, selling and producing abroad

Demographic factors

These include birth and death rates as well as the distribution of the age structure within a population. In many Western countries, falling birth rates mean that the population is declining. This may make these countries less attractive to businesses because the market size is getting smaller. Instead Western businesses may target emerging markets which have high birth rates and a larger proportion of younger people.

Exchange rates

The exchange rate measures the price of one currency in terms of another. If the exchange rate falls, this makes the price of exports to foreign customers cheaper. As a result this will encourage a domestic business to focus more on selling its products overseas.

Figure 12 The effects of a weak currency on German exports

Managing international businesses including pressures for local responsiveness and for cost reduction

Due to the growth in globalisation, it is much easier for businesses to operate internationally. This is known as **internationalisation**. The growth of internationalisation is due to improvements in communications, lower transport costs and economic growth in emerging markets. As a consequence, businesses now have to seriously consider what international strategies they need to adopt.

Bartlett and Ghoshal's international strategies

This theory identified two competing pressures that need to be considered when developing an international strategy. These are local responsiveness, which is the extent to which products/services need to be adapted to suit the local tastes of different countries, and cost reduction, which is the need to standardise products in order to gain economies of scale from large-scale production, as well as to maintain a consistent image across the world.

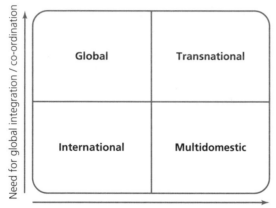

Figure 13 Bartlett and Ghoshal's international strategies

Bartlett and Ghoshal proposed that a business should adopt one of the following strategies:

- **Global strategy** – a centralised approach that involves large-scale production of identical products that are sold worldwide. For example, Airbus aircraft are identical, no matter which foreign airline buys them.
- **International strategy** – a centralised approach in which the majority of products are identical, but some are adapted to suit local tastes. For example, McDonald's restaurants around the world have the same layout, but may offer different food and drink products.
- **Multidomestic strategy** – a decentralised approach in which each branch is seen as a separate business and allowed to adapt the products specifically to the needs of its local population.
- **Transnational strategy** – different branches in each country specialise in a particular element of production, but work interdependently in order to produce the final product. For example, a global car manufacturer may produce identical engines in one country, but these can be used in a range of vehicles that are produced in other countries and are adapted to suit local tastes.

> **Internationalisation** means selling and/or operating in more than one country.

> **Knowledge check 14**
>
> Think of three ways that a car made by Ford could be adapted for the Indian market.

> **Exam tip**
>
> Bartlett and Ghoshal's international strategies are a new topic on the AQA specification.

The impact of internationalisation on the functional areas of a business

Marketing

It is vital that the marketing department fully understands the culture and tastes of the target market when selling in different countries. Extensive market research needs to be carried out and methods such as licensing and alliances with local businesses are valuable in gaining good understanding of consumer tastes.

People

Recruitment, selection and training of local staff is often key to being successful in international markets. This is because local employees understand the language and culture of the country. Senior managers need to take the time to understand the working practices and employment legislation for each of the countries the business operates in.

Operations

Outsourcing production usually provides cost-saving benefits. It also poses challenges, however, such as ensuring high quality and productivity and establishing contacts with new suppliers. Some Western businesses have been criticised for the poor working conditions in their overseas factories.

Finance

As well as the cost of international expansion, financial control becomes more difficult as a result of the business operating in several different countries. Economic factors such as inflation, interest rates, taxation and exchange rates make financial forecasting more difficult.

Exam tip

Questions on internationalisation will often require you to consider the opportunities for and threats to a business as a result of operating abroad. You may also be asked to decide on the best strategy for a business to adopt if it is to succeed in international markets.

Summary

From reading this section you should be able to:
- define internationalisation
- identify three reasons why a business would want to operate in international markets
- understand the different methods that a business can use to enter international markets
- explain the factors that influence the attractiveness of international markets
- define offshoring and re-shoring
- explain Bartlett and Ghoshal's theory of international strategies
- understand the importance of local responsiveness when operating in different countries
- identify two reasons why a business would offshore
- explain how internationalisation would affect the people function of a business
- understand the importance of cost reduction when operating in international markets.

Assessing greater use of digital technology

The pressures to adopt digital technology

The pressure to adopt **digital technology** stems from the greater profitability that a business can gain through its use. Revenue can be increased by the ability of technology to reach more customers and develop a better understanding of their buying habits. Efficiencies from the use of digital technology can produce significant cost savings.

Digital technology is the use of computer-based equipment and media. It includes the use of e-commerce, big data, data mining and enterprise resource planning (ERP).

Table 6 How digital technology helps to achieve the aim of boosting profits

Underlying aim: To boost profit		
Objective	**How to do it**	**Digital technology that enables this**
Boost revenue	Reach more customers Find out customer needs and address them Speedier, more accurate delivery	E-commerce Analysing data on consumer behaviour Enterprise resource planning
Reduce costs	Produce faster Lower overheads Reduce wastage	Computer-aided manufacturing, enterprise resource planning, plus use of robots in production Teleworking Enterprise resource planning

E-commerce

This is the process of selling goods and services online. Businesses no longer require actual stores to sell their products as customers instead order them directly through a website. Products are then delivered to the customer's address. Companies such as Amazon, ASOS and eBay are examples.

Big data

This is the use of computer software by businesses to store information on customers' buying habits and to develop customer profiles. This provides a valuable source of quantitative market research. For example, Google can provide businesses with detailed information regarding their potential target market.

Data mining

This is the use of big data for marketing promotions. By building up customer profiles, individual consumers can be targeted with specific offers based on their buying habits. This also allows the effectiveness of marketing campaigns to be more accurately measured.

Knowledge check 15

Consider three ways in which Amazon uses big data and data mining when a customer places an order.

Enterprise resource planning

Enterprise resource planning (ERP) is a system used by businesses to collect, store, manage and interpret data from different business functions. It helps to co-ordinate the different functions of a business. ERP:

- calculates how soon inventories will be used up and when to place new orders
- calculates how many staff are required to complete an order and how long it should take
- ensures that all the right physical, human and information resources are available in the right place and at the right time for the business to function effectively.

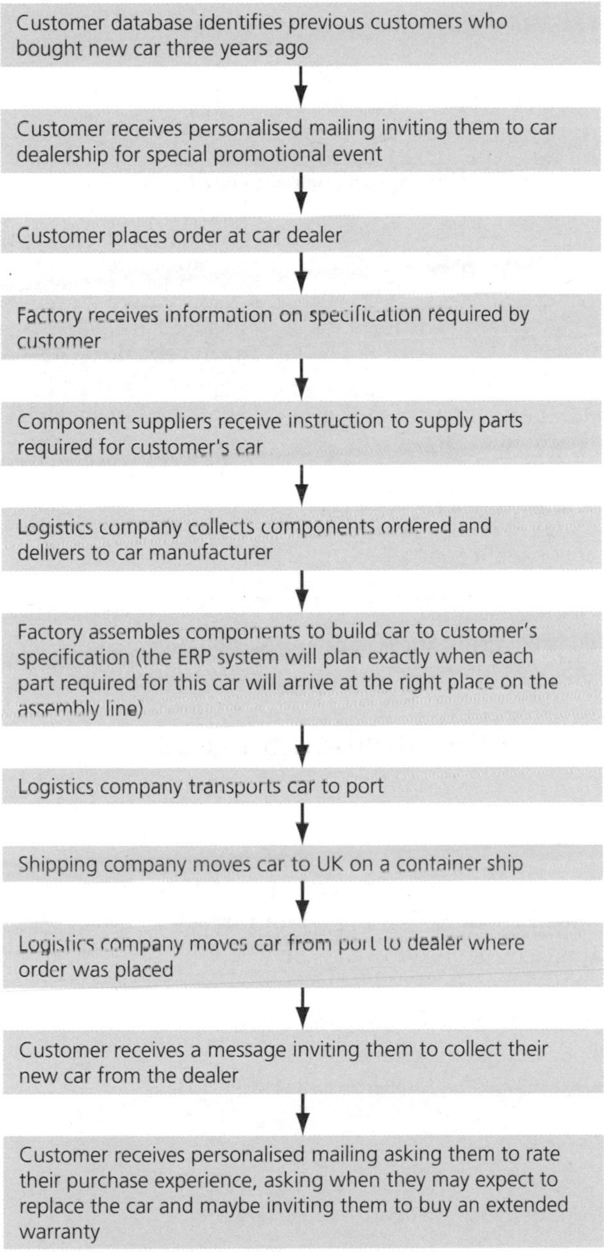

Customer database identifies previous customers who bought new car three years ago

↓

Customer receives personalised mailing inviting them to car dealership for special promotional event

↓

Customer places order at car dealer

↓

Factory receives information on specification required by customer

↓

Component suppliers receive instruction to supply parts required for customer's car

↓

Logistics company collects components ordered and delivers to car manufacturer

↓

Factory assembles components to build car to customer's specification (the ERP system will plan exactly when each part required for this car will arrive at the right place on the assembly line)

↓

Logistics company transports car to port

↓

Shipping company moves car to UK on a container ship

↓

Logistics company moves car from port to dealer where order was placed

↓

Customer receives a message inviting them to collect their new car from the dealer

↓

Customer receives personalised mailing asking them to rate their purchase experience, asking when they may expect to replace the car and maybe inviting them to buy an extended warranty

Figure 14 The stages in the ERP system

The value of digital technology

Digital technology can provide a competitive advantage for a business, particularly if its rivals are not using it as effectively. It provides significant cost savings, greater convenience for customers and better understanding of their buying habits. Many businesses have embraced digital technology as a valuable USP, for example Domino's Pizza developing a smartphone app for customers to place orders.

Introducing digital technology requires a significant initial investment in purchasing hardware and software, training staff and reorganising physical systems, however.

> **Knowledge check 16**
>
> Think of two reasons why a high-class fashion business would sell its clothes in a store rather than online.

Businesses may not be able to afford the cost of digital technology or may not believe that it is appropriate for their business model.

Table 7 The impact of e-commerce, data mining and ERP

E-commerce		Mining big data		ERP	
Makes product more accessible to customers		Can understand customers better	Increased cost of data analysis	Helps to spread information throughout the organisation	Substantial investment required in hardware and software
Boosts total size of potential market		Allows customer needs to be met more closely		Ensures decision making is based on most reliable up-to-date information available	
Can increase revenues	Higher spending on promotion trying to reach bigger market	May allow premium pricing and/or stronger customer loyalty		Should improve decision making and operational efficiency	
Need to invest in adjusting distribution network to service e-commerce, across a wider area		Will increased revenues outweigh extra cost of data analysis?		Ought to lower operating costs	
Will increased revenues outweigh extra costs?		But there may be ethical issues involved when firms know 'too much' about customers		How long will operating cost reductions take to outweigh initial investment in ERP?	

The impact of digital technology on the functional areas of a business

Marketing

Digital technology has a significant impact on marketing. E-commerce has transformed the way products are promoted and distributed. It is important that a business's website is constantly updated and is easy for customers to use when ordering online. Big data and data mining enable businesses to build up accurate customer profiles and identify trends in buying habits. Social media and electronic messaging provide valuable promotional methods to target consumers with personalised offers. The use of dynamic pricing enables businesses to alter their prices according to demand.

People

Staffing levels can be monitored electronically and adjusted according to customer demand. For example, Amazon knows from its records that demand will peak in the weeks leading up to Christmas. Extra employees can then be recruited to work in its warehouse in this period. Digital technology also means that staff with specialist IT skills need to be recruited for website design and software programming.

Operations

The need to maintain an effective logistics system, which ensures that customers get their products quickly and conveniently without excessive cost, is vital for successful e-commerce. The use of ERP has had a huge impact on operational systems, by improving co-ordination and communication.

Table 8 How ERP helps each functional area

Marketing	Provides up-to-the-minute sales figures via Electronic Point of Sale (EPOS) systems, such as the bar code scanners in supermarkets Gathers information on customer buying habits, often linked with a loyalty card system such as Tesco's Clubcard Can produce individually addressed promotional materials tailored to appeal to specific customers
Finance	Allows 'real-time' accounting information to be produced based on sales and costs incurred, generating financial information for individual profit centres or the whole business Allows budget variances to be analysed on a daily (or hourly) basis Some systems have the facility to conduct sensitivity analysis by pulling in data from other areas – such as how much profit would be generated from accepting a special order
HR	The payroll function (working out how much each staff member should be paid per month) can be an integrated component of an ERP system Staff rotas can be produced, based on predictions of demand that are generated by the analysis of past data on customer numbers for identical time periods
Operations	Production planning is perhaps the core function of a manufacturer's ERP system – working out how much to make of each type of product to satisfy demand, and identifying the most efficient sequence of production for different orders to minimise both customer waiting times and time spent adjusting machinery ERP systems offer logistical functions that can plan for what supplies need to be transported from source to destination and the most efficient way to do this in terms of both time and cost

Finance

Digital technology can be used for financial planning and budgetary control through the use of spreadsheets and databases. Investment in digital technology can be costly and ongoing in order to keep up with technological developments.

Exam tip

Digital technology is becoming increasingly important as a business tool. Questions on this topic may require you to evaluate the advantages and disadvantages for a business that arise from the use of digital technology.

Summary

From reading this section you should be able to:
- define digital technology
- identify at least two benefits of digital technology for business
- identify at least two problems resulting from the increased use of digital technology
- define e-commerce
- explain the value of big data and data mining

- understand how an ERP system works
- explain the impact of digital technology on the following functional areas:
  a marketing
  b operations
  c people
  d finance.

■ Managing strategic change

Managing change

Causes of and pressures for change

Types of change

Internal change is usually planned for as it starts from within the business, for example the setting of new objectives. External change is caused by factors outside the business and is often unexpected, such as changes in consumer tastes.

Table 9 Examples of internal and external causes of change

Internal causes	External causes
New growth objectives set by management New boss appointed Decision made to open up new export markets A decision to increase the shareholders' dividend makes it difficult to find the capital to invest in the business	Rising consumer demand/the product becomes fashionable Economic boom benefits luxury products Closure/fire/strike hits competitor, boosting your sales New laws favour your product (e.g. new safety laws boost sales of first aid kits)

Incremental change is predictable and can be planned for, for instance the increased popularity of e-commerce over the last few years. Disruptive change is unpredictable, occurs quickly and is difficult to plan for, for example the way the rapid growth and popularity of Uber has disrupted the taxi market.

Managing change – Lewin's force field analysis

Lewin identified that there are factors both in favour of and resistant to a proposed change. To manage change successfully, he identified the need to overcome resistant views to proposed change and encourage new working practices in order to implement it. The following steps need to be followed:

- Identify a problem or opportunity for change.
- Through consultation, identify all the views both for and against the change.
- Give each view a score in terms of its strength of argument.
- Add up the scores both for and against the change and decide which is the stronger.

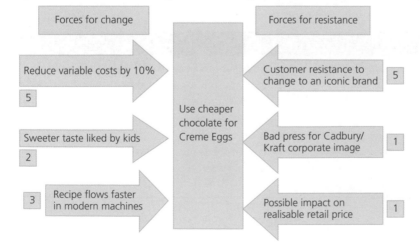

Figure 15 Making a case for and against change

Knowledge check 17

In the example in Figure 15, calculate the total scores both for change and for resistance. Based on these, would Cadbury's decide to implement the change of using cheaper chocolate for Creme Eggs?

Exam tip

Lewin's force field analysis is a new topic in the AQA specification.

The value of change

Most businesses dislike change. This is because it can be unpredictable and disruptive and is often resisted by employees.

Change often creates new business opportunities, however. It forces managers to think more creatively and to come up with new ideas for products and services. This means consumers may benefit from improved products, more choice and better service.

The value of a flexible organisation

Innovation

Flexible organisations are able to rapidly develop and supply new products in response to changes in consumer tastes. They tend to be more profitable because they can generate higher revenues and have lower costs. Higher revenues are gained because the business is consistently able to bring out new products to meet consumer tastes. This means that it always sells products that consumers want. Also, because they can launch new products before their rivals, flexible organisations benefit from 'first mover advantage'. Zara is a good example of a successful flexible business through its use of 'fast fashion'. This enables it quickly to identify the latest fashion trends and develop new products to meet customer tastes.

A **flexible organisation** is one that is able to change rapidly without loss of efficiency.

efficient use of tech

Flexible organisations are usually very efficient. They use production systems that can quickly switch from one product to another, reducing 'downtime'. They employ multi-skilled, productive 'core' workers on a permanent full-time basis, but during busy periods additional 'peripheral' workers are employed on temporary contracts, which end when the busy period is over. Consequently the business saves on labour costs as it employs workers only when they are needed.

Figure 16 Examples of a flexible organisation

Restructuring

This involves making savings by reorganising a business's operations through reducing its capacity. Typically this is achieved by **outsourcing**. Examples of business operations that can be outsourced include payroll, security and cleaning. The benefit of outsourcing is that it frees up business resources to be used for more profitable activities.

Outsourcing is when a business transfers work that it normally does itself to another business, which can usually do it more efficiently.

Delayering

This is when a business reduces the size of its organisational structure by removing layers of management. This reduces costs because the business employs fewer managers and supervisors. It also improves communication because the hierarchy between senior managers and the workforce is shortened. As a result, the time to implement strategic changes should be quicker because information does not have to pass through many layers of management.

Flexible employment contracts

These enable an employer to alter the size of its workforce and wage bill more rapidly in response to changes in consumer demand. These contracts are offered usually to peripheral workers. A good example is zero hours contracts, where workers are paid only the number of hours required by the employer according to how busy the business is.

Organic vs mechanistic structures

An organic structure is one that has flexibility and fluidity. It has a culture where change is expected and welcomed. Organic structures tend to be decentralised; employees work in empowered teams that are encouraged by senior managers to spot problems or identify opportunities and to come up with solutions. Examples of businesses with organic structures include Facebook and Microsoft.

Mechanistic structures are the opposite. They are centralised and all decision making is done by senior managers. Working practices and procedures are formalised and employees are expected simply to follow orders set by senior management. Examples include organisations such as the police and armed forces.

The value of managing information and knowledge

Information management involves how to cost-effectively collect and organise the data that a business needs to carry out its operations. By using sophisticated IT systems, this information can be instantly accessible and up to date, enabling improved decision making.

Knowledge management is about creating the right learning environment within a business so that vital information can be quickly shared among the workforce. It makes a business more flexible and innovative because it encourages the free flow of ideas between employees.

Barriers to change

There is a natural tendency for employees within a business to resist change. Before implementing change it is important for a business to identify the possible barriers to change.

Kotter and Schlesinger identified four reasons for resistance to change:

- **Parochial self-interest** – employees feel threatened by change because they fear that they may lose power and status, as well as worrying that their pay and conditions will become worse.
- **Misunderstanding** – this results from mistrust of senior management by employees. As a result the proposed change is viewed negatively.

Knowledge check 19

Find out what an 'annual hours' contract is.

- **Low tolerance** – most employees dislike change because they prefer security and stability. 'Fear of the unknown' is a common barrier to change.
- **Different assessments** – employees may take the view of 'If it's not broken, why fix it?' This means they consider that the business is working efficiently and consequently that there is no need for change. Senior managers may take a different view, however, due to the fact that they have access to more information and are better placed to consider whether improvements are necessary.

Table 10 Kotter and Schlesinger's barriers to change

Kotter and Schlesinger's four major barriers to change	
Parochial self-interest	Concern over how the change affects each individual, rather than the business as a whole
Misunderstanding	Of the details of the changes being implemented and how they will affect individuals
Low tolerance	Some individuals crave security and stability at work and thus have a naturally low tolerance to change
Different assessments	From staff who may believe the change is unnecessary or believe the drawbacks of the changes outweigh the benefits

How to overcome barriers to change

Kotter and Schlesinger identified six ways of overcoming resistance to change. They recommended that a mixture of these different methods should be used, depending on the nature of the workforce and the speed of the change.

- **Education and communication** – managers explain the reasons for the need for change before it is implemented.
- **Participation and involvement** – managers listen to the views of employees and take these into account when implementing the changes.
- **Facilitation and support** – managers should offer training and support for employees to overcome fear of change.
- **Negotiation and agreement** – managers offer an incentive in return for employees agreeing to the proposed changes. This could involve a bonus or pay rise.
- **Manipulation and co-option** – managers provide only limited information to those employees resisting change, or deliberately try to undermine their resistance.
- **Explicit and implicit coercion** – managers force employees to accept the proposed changes through threats, e.g. loss of jobs, limited promotion prospects if change is resisted.

Table 11 Summary of methods for overcoming resistance to change

	Advantages	Drawbacks	Use it when:
Education and communication	Builds commitment to the change once staff understand what is needed and why	Time consuming and expensive	Resistors lack information or understanding of the proposed change
Participation and involvement	The best way of building commitment as staff feel ownership of changes that they have had a hand in designing	Consultation is a time-consuming process; there is a danger of poor decision making from staff who may not have all available information	Change designers lack information that staff could provide
Facilitation and support	Especially good at dealing with low tolerance change resistors	Can take time, be expensive and still fail	The major cause of resistance is difficulty in adjusting to new methods

> **Exam tip**
>
> Kotter and Schlesinger's theory of change management is a new topic in the AQA specification.

> **Knowledge check 20**
>
> A business wishes to introduce a new IT system. Which of Kotter and Schlesinger's methods would you use to overcome any resistance to this change?

	Advantages	Drawbacks	Use it when:
Negotiation and agreement	Can be an effective way of gaining compliance of all who will be negatively affected	Can be expensive to make concessions and may alert others to the benefit of resisting	A powerful group will lose out from the change
Manipulation and co-option	Can work quickly and be done cheaply	May leave staff feeling manipulated – damaging employer–employee relations going forward	Other methods will not work or are too costly
Explicit and implicit coercion	Can be done quickly and overcome any type of resistance in the short term	Leads to only grudging acceptance of changes and creates ill will that is likely to persist in the future	Speed is vital and those driving change are powerful

Summary

From reading this section you should be able to:
- understand the difference between internal and external change
- define disruptive change
- explain Lewin's force field analysis
- identify two reasons why change is valuable for a business
- define the term 'flexible organisation'
- understand restructuring, delayering and flexible employment contracts
- explain the differences between an organic and a mechanistic structure
- understand the value of managing information and knowledge
- identify Kotter and Schlesinger's four reasons for resistance to change
- understand Kotter and Schlesinger's six ways of overcoming resistance to change.

Managing organisational culture

The importance of organisational culture

Organisational culture is often described as 'the way we do things round here'. It develops over time as a result of: the aims or mission of the business; the behaviour of senior managers; the attitude of senior management to enterprise and risk; and the recruitment and training procedures.

Culture is essential for business success. Common characteristics of the companies in the *Sunday Times*' '100 best companies to work for' include:
- a genuine focus on customers' needs
- an enterprising 'can do' attitude among all staff
- a long-term commitment to the business
- a belief among staff that the business is making a positive contribution to the economy and to society.

Handy's four types of culture

Handy identified four types of culture:
- **Task** – based on the successful completion of specific projects. Projects are assigned to teams made up of individuals from different functional areas. Power and authority is based on the level of expertise that each team member brings to the project.

> **Organisational culture** is the attitudes, behaviour and ethos of the workforce.

- **Role** – often found in bureaucratic organisations that have formal procedures for completing activities. Power and authority is based on an individual's position within the organisation. A role culture is typically found in organisations such as the police and armed forces.
- **Power** – authority is concentrated in one person or among a small group of individuals at the top of the organisation. This is often found in organisations where there is a powerful, autocratic leader who makes all the key decisions. When Steve Jobs was in charge of Apple, the business was said to have a power culture.
- **Person** – developed among individuals with similar levels of education and experience and from similar backgrounds, who are encouraged to form groups in order to enhance their expertise and share knowledge. It is often found in specialist departments within large organisations, such as IT or legal staff.

Hofstede's national cultures

Hofstede identified four categories of culture:

- **Power distance** – the degree to which workers feel it is acceptable for there to be a big distance between themselves and senior management.
- **Individualism–collectivism** – how much power should be given to individuals rather than collectively to groups of workers.
- **Uncertainty avoidance** – the degree to which workers prefer to be cautious rather than risk-taking.
- **Masculinity–femininity** – the extent to which workers prefer fact-based decision making (male) compared to intuitive decision making (female).

Hofstede's research found that workers from different countries would differ in terms of the four categories of culture, as shown in Table 12.

Table 12 Differences between national cultures using Hofstede's main measures

	Power distance	Individualism	Uncertainty avoidance	Masculinity/femininity
Canada	39	80	48	52
China	80	20	30	66
Denmark	18	74	23	16
France	68	71	86	43
Germany	35	67	65	66
India	77	48	40	56
Mexico	81	30	82	69
Netherlands	38	80	53	14
Poland	68	60	93	64
South Korea	60	18	85	39
United Kingdom	35	89	35	66
United States	40	91	46	62
Mean average	58	49	65	50

Source: Geert Hofstede, *Culture's Consequences: International Differences in Work-Related Values*, Beverly Hills, CA, 1980

Increased internationalisation makes Hofstede's work valuable, as businesses that employ workers from different countries can gain a greater understanding of their preferred working practices.

Knowledge check 21

What type of culture do you think would be adopted by a pharmaceutical business developing new medicines?

Knowledge check 22

Using Table 12, identify the preferred culture of workers from the Netherlands, according to Hofstede.

The influences on organisational culture

Leadership

Culture is often determined by the personality and leadership style of the founder of the business. For example, businesses such as Facebook and Google have a culture that reflects the 'laissez-faire' leadership style of their founders, namely Mark Zuckerberg, Larry Page and Sergei Brin respectively. Other businesses have leaders who prefer a more autocratic approach; Sir Philip Green, the owner of Arcadia, is a good example.

Type of ownership

Public limited companies (plc's) are owned by shareholders who expect them to provide rising dividends and share price. This may result in the business adopting a 'short-termist' culture, with the emphasis being on making high profits quickly.

Private limited companies tend to be family-owned and usually can take a longer-term view. Consequently there is less pressure to make quick profits in these businesses.

Type of workforce

If senior management lacks diversity, it may produce a culture that is 'out of touch' with the rest of the workforce and with its customers. For example, the majority of executives in the UK's top companies are male, white and middle aged.

The reasons for and problems of changing organisational culture

Reasons for change include:

- **Changes in the external environment** – examples could include new competition, changes in consumer tastes, or economic, technological and environmental factors.
- **Poor business performance** – falling profitability, sales revenue and market share. Often this results in a new leader being appointed to change the culture of a business in order to improve its performance.

Problems of changing organisational culture include:

- **Resistance from employees** – especially from staff who have worked for the business for a long time. They may fear possible redundancy or having to learn new skills.
- **Length of time** – achieving cultural change may take several years, particularly if the existing culture has been in place for a long time.
- **Gaining support from senior management** – if senior management does not support the change in culture, it will be difficult for it to be accepted by all employees.

> **Exam tip**
>
> This section contains two new theories in the AQA specification. When answering questions on culture, showing knowledge of these theories is a good way to gain marks for analysis.

Summary

From reading this section you should be able to:

- define organisational culture
- understand why culture is important for business success
- explain Handy's task, role, power and person cultures

- understand Hofstede's national cultures
- identify two influences on business culture
- understand two reasons for the need to change culture
- identify two problems a business may face when changing culture.

Managing strategic implementation

How to implement strategy effectively

Before a strategy is **implemented**, the strategic goals that the businesses wishes to achieve must be established. SWOT analysis is a useful technique as it may enable a business to set strategic goals such as using its strengths to exploit an opportunity, for example using a strong brand name to enter new markets.

A firm's ability to execute strategic implementation effectively is one of the most important factors affecting organisational success. The business must identify:

- the activities that need to be completed in order to implement the strategy
- how these activities will be carried out
- which employees will be assigned to each activity
- when each activity will need to be completed by.

Strategic implementation involves putting plans into action, so that an organisation can achieve its goals. A good plan will not guarantee success; it needs to be put into practice and executed properly.

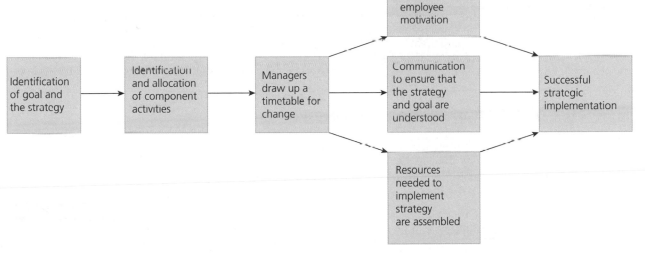

Figure 17 Effective strategic implementation

The value of leadership in strategic implementation

Strong leadership is crucial for the effective implementation of strategy. One of the biggest challenges a leader faces is convincing the workforce that strategic change is necessary. To implement strategy effectively the leader needs to:

- ensure that all employees understand the need for strategic change
- construct a clear vision about the future direction of the business and how it will be achieved
- appoint the right managers to execute the strategy and ensure that they are given the necessary support and resources from senior management
- be prepared to persist with the strategy and overcome any short-term difficulties that may arise.

Different leaders adopt different leadership styles when implementing strategy, as shown in Table 13.

Table 13 Leadership styles and the process of change

	Autocratic	Paternalistic	Democratic	Laissez-faire
Understand the scope of the change needed	Leader hires a management consultant who reports directly to him or her	Leader carries out an extensive consultation exercise among staff, based on the known issues or problems	Discussion and consultation is delegated to middle managers, taking care to include shop floor staff	A laissez-faire organisation may have been ahead of the external change, or may only react very late
Construct a clear vision	The management consultant writes a Vision Statement	This, again, will be done after consultation, though the leader makes the final decision	This should emerge, perhaps from suggestions from the shop floor	A laissez-faire leader may expect staff to grasp the vision as things emerge
Appoint change managers	Either management consultants or internal appointees who are used to doing what the boss wants	These are appointed from among known 'team players': that is, those who buy into the vision decided by the leader	These are selected from the brightest and best throughout the organisation	This is unlikely to happen; it will be expected that everyone will change over time
Keep going through short-term problems	Any internal critics may be sidelined or 'made redundant'	When things get tough, the leader draws upon tough, family love and the need to stick together	If everyone shares the vision and has agreed the strategy, this stage should not be a real problem	Because the change is less controlled and therefore slower and more organic, this problem may not occur

The value of communications in strategic implementation

Strategic decisions are usually made by senior managers, and are then passed down to the other employees in the business. Good communication is essential to ensure that the new strategy is fully understood by all employees. If the workforce do not understand the strategy, they will also probably not know what is expected of them and what they are supposed to be doing. As a result the new strategy could fail.

Senior managers need to ensure that they are visible to all staff and that they communicate directly with them. It is important that they empower departmental managers with the authority to decide how best to implement the strategy within their own functional areas.

The importance of organisational structure in strategic implementation

Types of organisational structure

In functional organisational structures, employees are organised into functional departments. The advantage of this type of structure is that employees with specialist skills can be grouped together. This can result in better productivity and quality. The disadvantage is that departments may work in isolation from each other and this lack of co-operation may lead to destructive departmental rivalries.

Knowledge check 23

Identify the four stages of effective strategic implementation.

A firm's **organisational structure** describes how it is set up and organised. Organisational charts show the different layers of management that make up a firm's hierarchy. They also show lines of authority and channels of communication.

Figure 18 Organisational structure by function

Product-based organisational structures are used by businesses that make a range of different products. The business splits itself into different divisions, and each division specialises in producing a particular product. For example, Samsung has separate divisions for its televisions, smartphones and digital recording products. Each division has its own functional structure.

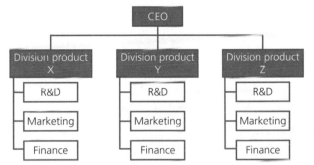

Figure 19 Organisational structure by product

The advantage of this type of structure is that each division can specialise and work independently. This, however, may lead to each division working towards its specific goals rather than towards those of the overall business.

A regional organisational structure is similar to a product-based organisation in that it is sub-divided into separate divisions. The divisions are based on geographical locations. For example, a ferry company may have a regional structure based on the different destinations its ferries go to, such as Scandinavia or the Mediterranean.

The advantage of this structure is that each division has more independence and a better understanding of its specific consumer tastes, meaning that it can adapt the product accordingly. Similar to a product-based organisation, however, each division may focus on its own goals rather than on those of the business as a whole.

In a matrix organisational structure, employees from different specialist areas work together in multi-disciplinary teams. This is usually for specific projects, for example a car company may set up a project team consisting of designers, engineers and marketing specialists in order to develop a new model.

The benefits of a matrix structure include greater sharing of ideas and co-operation between functional areas. This should lead to better problem solving and quicker development of new products. A disadvantage is that each member of the project team may face a conflict of interests between their own department and the project they are working on.

Organisational structure is important in strategic implementation because it determines which staff are involved in the specific activities that make up the overall strategy. Furthermore, strategic implementation may require a change in organisational structure. For example, a business that wishes to enter new markets may need to change from a product-based to a matrix structure, especially if some of its existing products are failing.

Knowledge check 24

Identify one advantage and one disadvantage of a functional organisational structure.

Exam tip

Strategic implementation is a topic often used for essay questions. Try and include in your answers examples of businesses that have experienced strategic implementation.

The value of network analysis in strategic implementation

Network analysis is a way of showing how a complex project can be completed in the shortest possible time. It identifies the activities that must be completed on time to avoid delaying the whole project. It is a valuable technique for strategic implementation, as it enables managers to construct a day-to-day plan that shows workers exactly what they should be doing, as well as when and how.

A network diagram shows:

- the order in which tasks must be undertaken
- how long each task should take
- the earliest time at which each task can start.

A network diagram consists of two components:

1 The activities required to complete the overall project.
2 Nodes that represent the start or finish of a particular activity. All network diagrams start and end with a node.

In the example in Figure 20, all the different activities necessary for the completion of the project have been identified, as well as how long each one will take and in which order.

> Network analysis enables a business to identify the critical path, which is the activities that need to be monitored closely by management to ensure that the project is completed efficiently and on time.

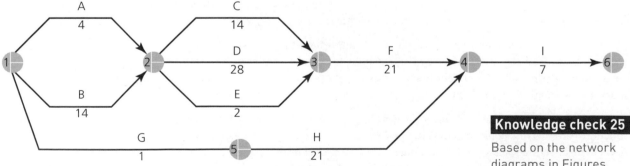

Figure 20 Network diagram for a '3p-off price promotion' (1)

The network diagram in Figure 21 shows the activities represented by letters and the nodes by numbers.

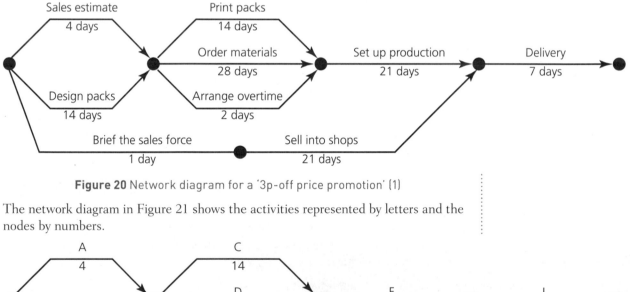

Figure 21 Network diagram for a '3p-off price promotion' (2)

Knowledge check 25

Based on the network diagrams in Figures 20 and 21, what is the shortest time that the project can take to be completed?

Each node contains a number as well as an earliest start time (EST) and latest finishing time (LFT). Each EST shows the earliest time that an activity can be started. The network diagram in Figure 22 shows the ESTs for all the activities.

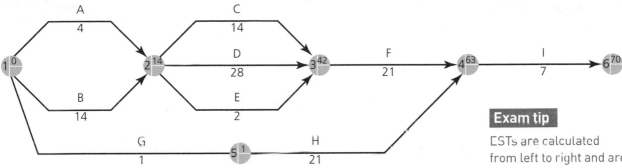

Figure 22 Network diagram for a '3p-off price promotion' (3)

Calculation of ESTs is important for identifying when resources such as staff, machinery and raw materials need to be ready. It enables a business to make efficient use of resources, e.g. inventories, as stock is ordered only when required. Calculation of ESTs is also important for calculating the earliest time that the whole project can be completed (the EST in the final node).

Latest finishing times (LFT) show the latest time by which an activity must be completed. LFTs are recorded in the bottom right-hand section of the node and indicate the latest finishing time of the preceding activity. They are calculated from right to left. The network diagram in Figure 23 shows the LFTs for each activity.

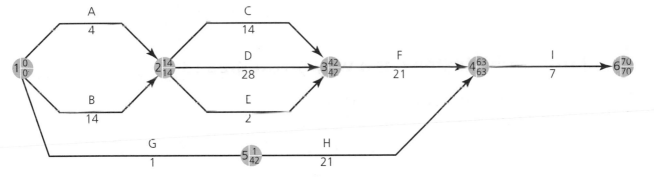

Figure 23 Network diagram for a '3p-off price promotion' (4)

Calculation of LFTs is important for providing deadlines that must be met for the project to be completed on time, for identifying activities that have 'float' time (see below) and for identifying the critical path (see below).

The critical path

This comprises the activities that take the longest to complete. They determine the length of the whole project and pass through nodes where the EST and LFT are equal. These activities are critical because they do not have any float time. If they are delayed, the whole project will miss its deadline.

The critical path therefore allows managers to focus their attention on ensuring that these activities are completed on time. If there is a danger that they could be delayed, resources from non-critical activities can be re-deployed to ensure that the critical activities meet their LFTs.

Total float

Float is the spare time available for the completion of an activity. It is calculated using the formula:

Float = LFT – duration – EST

For example, in the network diagram above, the total float for activity C would be:

42 – 14 – 14 = 14

Amendment of network diagrams

It must always be remembered that network diagrams are useful for planning projects, but in reality unexpected events may mean that activities take longer than estimated. As a result it is important that a business has the flexibility to amend its network diagram in response to these events.

Knowledge check 27

Calculate the total float for activity E.

Exam tip

Questions on network diagrams may require you to recalculate the critical path as a result of an activity taking longer than planned.

Summary

From reading this section you should be able to:
- define strategic implementation
- understand the importance of leadership for strategic implementation
- explain why communication is important for strategic implementation

- understand the difference between functional, product-based, regional and matrix organisational structures
- define what a network diagram is
- understand how to calculate ESTs and LFTs
- identify the critical path
- calculate and understand the significance of 'total float'.

Problems with strategy and why strategies fail

Difficulties of strategic decision making and implementing strategy

Its strategy is the way in which a business attempts to achieve its objectives. Strategic decision making has a long-term impact on the business and cannot easily be reversed. The difficulty with strategic decision making and implementing strategy is that changes in the external environment are difficult to predict. As a result, even a well-planned strategy may fail.

For example, until recently supermarkets such as Tesco and Sainsbury's based their expansion plans on opening more large stores on the outskirts of towns. Customers' increasing preference to make frequent shopping trips to smaller town centre stores, however, combined with the growth of online shopping, meant that the plans to open larger stores had to be cancelled.

Planned vs emergent strategy

All strategies are planned in advance by the directors of a business. A planned strategy will be well organised, have specific objectives and consist of a series of actions that are based on extensive market research. A criticism of planned strategies, however, is that they assume market conditions are stable. Consequently, if unanticipated changes occur in the external environment, a planned strategy is too inflexible to respond.

As a result of this, many business theorists now argue that businesses should instead adopt emergent strategies, particularly in response to the increasing rate of change in the external environment. An emergent strategy is one that is flexible and responsive to changing circumstances. Strategy emerges as a result of changes in the external environment rather than being controlled and rigid. Consequently businesses now have to be more intuitive and quick-thinking.

Reasons for strategic drift

The main reason for **strategic drift** is lack of attention from senior management. They may become too focused on other issues and neglect to monitor the progress of the main strategy. An example would be Nokia, which dominated the mobile phone market for several years, but failed to change its strategy quickly enough in response to the rapid popularity of Apple's iPhone.

The possible effect of the divorce of ownership and control

Public limited companies are owned by shareholders. They appoint the directors of the business, who control it on their behalf. The directors are expected to run the business efficiently and to devise strategies that improve the profitability of the business. Shareholders expect to benefit from improved profitability through good dividend payments and a rising share price.

The difficulty is that sometimes the directors have different objectives from those of the shareholders, for instance they may be more interested in job security and receiving high bonus payments. As a result they may devise strategies that meet their objectives rather than those of the shareholders. For example, Barclays bank has in the past been criticised for awarding some of its senior employees huge bonuses, rather than giving this money to shareholders or reinvesting it back into the business.

To avoid this situation arising, businesses need to ensure that they have effective corporate governance. This means that the activities of the board of directors are carefully monitored to ensure that it is acting in the best interests of the shareholders. The chairman of the company has ultimate responsibility for ensuring that the chief executive is behaving properly.

Evaluating strategic performance

This involves measuring whether the strategy has achieved its stated objectives, such as increasing profits or market share. If objectives are not SMART, however, they may be difficult to evaluate. Furthermore, strategic performance needs to be measured over a reasonably long time frame, usually three to five years. A strategy may generate short-term success, but may damage the business in the long term. For example, a business may cut costs by reducing spending on research and development, which could boost profits in the short term but cause long-term damage due to a possible lack of new product development.

The value of strategic planning

Strategic planning is essential for businesses because it forces them to plan how strategic decisions will be carried out – for example, through undertaking market research and completing a SWOT analysis – and to establish a time frame for the strategy, set objectives and identify what resources are required.

Knowledge check 28

Would a planned or emergent strategy be best for a company such as Google? Give a reason why.

Strategic drift means allowing a failing strategy to continue.

Knowledge check 29

Do you remember what the acronym SMART stands for?

Strategic planning has an opportunity cost, however, in that it takes time and money. This is particularly true in fast-changing markets. If a business takes too long collecting and analysing data, the danger is that it will get left behind and decide on an inappropriate strategy.

Strategic planning is appropriate in stable markets and where a business has some control over its situation. In unstable, fast-changing markets, an emergent strategy may be more appropriate.

The value of contingency planning

Contingency planning involves a business considering 'what if' scenarios and coming up with ways to deal with them. It enables the business to consider what actions would need to be taken if a particular threat emerges. This planning can minimise the potential damage that the threat could cause.

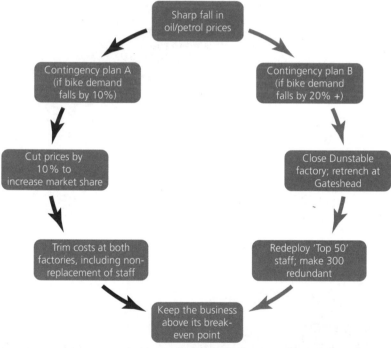

Figure 24 The process of contingency planning

Contingency planning is essential in an uncertain world where many potential threats can occur.

Summary

From reading this section you should be able to:

- identify one reason why strategic decision making is difficult
- explain the difference between a planned and an emergent strategy
- define the term 'strategic drift'
- understand the difficulty that can result from the divorce of ownership and control
- explain the importance of corporate governance
- identify two difficulties in evaluating strategic performance
- understand one advantage and one disadvantage of strategic planning
- define contingency planning.

Questions & Answers

AQA A-level Business consists of three exam papers.

Paper 1 consists of four compulsory sections:

- Section A: 15 multiple choice questions (15 marks in total).
- Section B: short-answer questions (35 marks in total).
- Sections C and D: two essay questions (each section offers a choice of one question from two), each worth 25 marks (50 marks in total).

Paper 2:

- Three data-response compulsory questions, worth approximately 33 marks each and made up of three- or four-part questions (100 marks in total).

Paper 3:

- An extended case study including appendices containing data: six questions of increasing levels of difficulty (100 marks in total).

This section of the guide contains the various types of exam questions that you are likely to be faced with. The exam papers can contain questions from the entire specification. The questions in this guide are based on all the sections in the specification. **Remember that the sections covered in this book – 'Strategic methods: how to pursue strategies' and 'Managing strategic change' – may be examined in all three papers.** The correct answers for the multiple choice questions are supplied in this section, together with comments on why these answers are correct. For the short-answer, data-response, case study and essay questions you will find sample answers with comments. The Student A sample answers are good responses and the Student B answers are weak responses; the aim is to illustrate common errors made by students and give examples of good practice in the hope that you will, with practice, be able to develop your own skills.

Questions

Since the multiple choice and short-answer questions give a broad coverage of the content of this book, it would make sense to use these towards the end of your revision period in order to check your knowledge. The data-response questions, however, could be used as you complete an area of content. The Paper 3 questions are based on different content sections of the entire specification, but would be best answered towards the end of your revision. Note that the example given in this guide for Paper 3 has three questions totalling 48 marks, which is fewer than the six questions (worth 100 marks) that you will find in the exam.

Sample answers

Resist the temptation to study the answers before you have attempted the questions. If you make a mistake here, it is not the end of the world and practising developing your own responses will help you hone your skills. Once you have written your answer, you can then look at the sample responses and identify the strengths and weaknesses of your own work. Using the Question & Answer section in this way should result in the quality of your answers improving.

Assessment

A-level papers do not just test how well you know the content of the subject. There is a clear set of skills that will be tested and it is essential that you are aware of these skills and have some idea how to satisfy them.

The following skills are tested:

- **Knowledge and understanding** – this relates to the content of the specification and how well you know and understand the various business concepts, theories and ideas.
- **Application** – this focuses on your ability to relate your knowledge and understanding of the subject content to a particular situation or scenario (such as that given in a particular case study).
- **Analysis** – this is the ability to develop an extended line of argument related to a particular question.
- **Evaluation** – making a judgement by weighing up the evidence provided.

It is important to understand that not all questions test all of the skills set out above and as a result it is important that you are able to recognise which skills are being tested by each question. The basis of all questions will be some element of knowledge, but what other skills will be required? The clue to this is in the command words of a question. Some commonly used ones are illustrated below.

Application

The following command words require you to apply your answer to the context of the question or case:

- 'Explain…'
- 'Calculate…'

Analyse

The following command words require you to develop a relevant argument. Remember that this also has to be in context and will also need application:

- 'Analyse…'
- 'Explain why…'
- 'Examine…'

Evaluate

The following command words require you to make a judgement. Remember again that in an answer that requires evaluation, arguments must be developed (analysis) and they must also be in context (application):

- 'Evaluate…'
- 'Discuss…'
- 'To what extent…'
- 'Justify…'

It is worth remembering that the majority of students who have studied Business seriously and who underperform do so not because of a lack of knowledge but because of a lack of good examination technique. If you understand the skills that are being tested, recognise how to develop them and are prepared to practise them, you will be one step ahead of the game.

Paper 1-type questions

Section A: Multiple choice questions

Question 1

Which one of the following is not a fixed cost?

A Rent

B Insurance

C Raw materials

D Salaries

Question 2

What is market capitalisation?

A The total value of a market.

B How much capital a business has raised.

C The total value of all the companies in the FTSE 100.

D The total value of a particular business.

Question 3

A product is achieving a high and stable level of sales. Which stage of the product life cycle is it in?

A Maturity

B Growth

C Decline

D Introduction

Question 4

Kotter and Schlesinger identified four reasons for resistance to change. Which one of the following is not a reason?

A Job security

B Misunderstanding

C Parochial self-interest

D Low tolerance

Question 5

The income elasticity of demand for a brand of perfume is +2. If incomes rose by 3%:

A   Quantity demanded would rise and sales revenue would fall.

B   Quantity demanded would rise and sales revenue would rise.

C   Quantity demanded would fall and sales revenue would rise.

D   Quantity demanded would fall and sales revenue would fall.

Question 6

A new piece of machinery costs £10 million. It is expected to last 3 years and generate a net return each year of £5 million. Using the following 10 per cent discount factors: Year 1 0.909, Year 2 0.826 and Year 3 0.751, the net present value is:

A   £5 million

B   £12.43 million

C   £2.43 million

D   £7 million

Question 7

Which one of the following best describes the term 'continuous improvement'?

A   Benchmarking

B   Kaizen

C   TQM

D   JIT

Question 8

Which one of the following is an example of fiscal policy to help business expansion?

A   Reduce interest rates

B   Quantitative easing

C   Encourage bank lending

D   Reduce corporation tax rates

Question 9

Extracts from the financial accounts of a company show:

Revenue	£200 million
Cost of sales	£75 million
Expenses	£50 million
Tax	£10 million

The business made an operating profit of:

A £125 million

B £75 million

C £65 million

D £40 million

Question 10

Bartlett and Ghoshal identified four different international strategies. A strategy based on decentralisation and localisation would be classified as:

A Multidomestic

B International

C Transnational

D Global

Question 11

A car manufacturer taking over an engine supplier would be an example of:

A Conglomerate integration

B Horizontal integration

C Forward vertical integration

D Backward vertical integration

Question 12

Which one of the following is not an example of digital technology?

A E-commerce

B Big data

C Decision trees

D ERP

Question 13

In a network diagram, Task E has an EST of 10 days, an LFT of 17 days and a duration of 3 days. Its total float is:

A 4 days

B 10 days

C 7 days

5 days

Question 14

Making an organisational structure flatter by reducing its length of hierarchy is known as:

A   Re-structuring

B   Delayering

C   Matrix

D   Decentralisation

Question 15

Data for a manufacturer shows:

	2015	2016
Possible output	100,000 units	100,000 units
Actual output	70,000 units	80,000 units
Number of workers	100	150

Which one of the following statements is correct?

A   Capacity utilisation has increased and labour productivity has increased.

B   Capacity utilisation has increased and labour productivity has decreased.

C   Capacity utilisation has decreased and labour productivity has decreased.

D   Capacity utilisation has decreased and labour productivity has increased.

Answers to multiple choice questions

Question 1

Correct answer C.

e Raw materials are a variable cost.

Question 2

Correct answer D.

e Market capitalisation is the total value of a business calculated by share price × number of shares.

Question 3

Correct answer A.

e Maturity – sales have peaked and remain at a high level.

Question 4

Correct answer A.

e Job security – this could be considered part of parochial self-interest, which is when workers fear loss of status.

Question 5

Correct answer B.

e Positive income elasticity of demand means that quantity and sales will increase with rising incomes.

Question 6

Correct answer C.

e £12.43 million – £10 million.

Question 7

Correct answer B.

e Kaizen is when a business is consistently focused on making minor improvements to the way it operates.

Question 8

Correct answer D.

e Fiscal policy consists of government spending and taxation decisions.

Question 9

Correct answer B.

e Operating profit = revenue – cost of sales – expenses.

Question 10

Correct answer A.

e Multidomestic strategy involves allowing the local branch of the business in a particular country to modify the product to meet its specific customer tastes.

Question 11

Correct answer D.

e The car manufacturer is taking over a business in the previous stage of the production chain.

Question 12

Correct answer C.

e Decision trees are a decision-making technique that does not necessarily require digital technology.

Question 13

Correct answer A.

ⓔ Total float = LFT – duration – EST.

Question 14

Correct answer B.

ⓔ Delayering involves removing layers of management from the hierarchy.

Question 15

Correct answer B.

ⓔ Capacity utilisation has increased from 70 per cent to 80 per cent, but labour productivity has fallen from 700 units per worker to 533.33 units.

Section B: Short-answer questions

Question 16

Look at this inventory control chart.

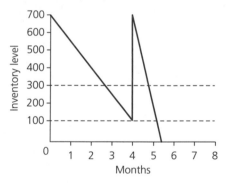

Based on the inventory control chart, answer **Questions 16(a), 16(b)** and **16(c)**.

(a) Calculate the average monthly level of sales between month 1 and month 4.   (2 marks)

ⓔ 'Calculate' questions simply require you to perform a calculation. It is important to show your workings as you may get marks for them even if your final answer is incorrect.

(b) If the re-order level is 300, calculate the lead time.   (2 marks)

(c) Explain **one** possible reason why inventory levels fell to zero between months 5 and 6.   (3 marks)

ⓔ 'Explain' questions require you to identify a point and then write a sentence that develops this point.

Student A

(a) Total sales between months 1 and 4 = 700 – 100 = 600

Average monthly sales = 600/4 = 150

e **2/2 marks awarded.** Correct calculations and workings shown.

Student B

(a) Total sales were 600.

e **1/2 marks awarded.** Correct figure for total sales (but no workings shown). Monthly sales figure not calculated.

Student A

(b) Inventory is re-ordered after approximately 2 months and 3 weeks. Arrives at the end of month 4. Lead time is 1 month and 1 week.

e **2/2 marks awarded.** Correct understanding of lead time and calculation.

Student B

(b) Lead time is the time between placing the order and when it arrives.

e **1/2 marks awarded.** Correct understanding of lead time, but no calculation offered.

Student A

(c) One possible reason was that there could have been an unexpected increase in demand. This is shown in the chart, which indicates that 700 units were sold in 6 weeks, meaning that the business was unable to order extra inventory to supply this demand.

e **3/3 marks awarded.** Valid reason identified and well explained using the data in the chart to illustrate the reason.

Student B

(c) The business could have failed to order the inventory on time.

e **1/3 marks awarded.** Valid reason but no explanation.

Question 17

Explain one possible benefit for a food manufacturing business that adopts a strategy of innovation. (4 marks)

e This question asks you to explain one benefit of innovation using the context of a food manufacturer. Try to think of a relevant example to illustrate your answer.

Innovation could result in new ideas for products or processes. A food manufacturer could benefit from a more efficient system to make its products. This could reduce wastage and improve productivity.

ⓔ **4/4 marks awarded.** Good understanding of innovation, as well as a relevant benefit identified and explained.

Innovation means coming up with new ideas. A food manufacturer could bring out a new popular product.

ⓔ **2/4 marks awarded.** Some understanding of innovation plus a relevant point made but not explained.

Question 18

The net gain for a business investing in new machinery is £5.5m. Referring to the decision tree, calculate the expected value and net gain of increasing the training budget. Using these calculations, advise the business which one of the two options it should choose. Show your workings.

(6 marks)

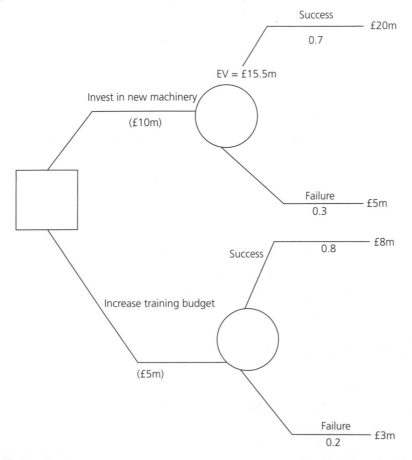

e This question requires you to calculate the expected value and net gain for the training budget. Remember to show your workings and, based on your calculations, advise which option to choose.

Student A

Expected value for the training budget:

$(0.8 \times 8) + (0.2 \times 3) = 6.4 + 0.6 = 7$

Net gain of increasing training budget = 7 – 5 = £2m

Net gain of investing in new machinery = £5.5m

Choose new machinery because it generates a higher net gain.

---

e **6/6 marks awarded.** Correct calculation with workings shown. Correct option chosen and justified.

Student B

Expected value for training budget = 8 + 3 – 5 = £6m

Expected value for new machinery is £5.5m.

Choose the training budget.

---

e **3/6 marks awarded.** Incorrect calculation of the training budget's expected value. 'Own figure rule' applies, however, so a mark awarded for the correct option based upon the calculations.

Question 19

Companies such as Google and Facebook claim that much of their success is due to their organisational culture. Analyse how an effective culture can improve the competitiveness of a business.

(9 marks)

e 'Analyse' questions require you to develop a line of argument. You should aim to write at least two consecutive sentences that provide a well-developed chain of argument with no missing links. You should also aim to write in context by applying your argument to the type of business featured in the question.

Student A

Organisational culture is the way that employees within a business behave and the attitudes they adopt within the workplace. Culture is often described as 'the way we do things around here'.

Culture can play a significant part in the competitiveness of a business because it directly affects how well employees perform their jobs. Both Google and Facebook have a reputation for a relaxed working culture, with senior managers adopting a 'laissez faire' leadership style. This culture works because these companies mainly employ skilled and creative employees, who expect to be

---

given the freedom to make their own decisions. Consequently employee morale is high. This results in improved competitiveness because the business should benefit from high productivity, low labour turnover and less absenteeism. In the case of companies like Google, the most significant benefit is that they retain a highly skilled and creative workforce, who consistently come up with new product ideas such as Google Maps and Gmail. This enables Google to retain its dominant position within its market.

ⓔ **9/9 marks awarded.** This is an excellent response. It reveals good understanding of the concept of culture. Relevant benefits resulting from an effective culture are identified and well explained. High application marks would be gained by using the business context of Google and Facebook to illustrate the points made.

Student B

Culture is the way that employees within a business behave. It can include things like what hours they work and the dress code.

Culture is important for competitiveness because it affects how employees deal with customers. John Lewis has a good reputation for customer service. This is because employees are well treated with benefits such as a profit share scheme. Good customer service means that John Lewis has a good reputation and will make high sales and profits.

ⓔ 4/9 marks awarded. This answer shows some understanding of culture. It identifies a relevant benefit using the example of John Lewis, but fails to explain in sufficient detail how culture contributes to good customer service. There is no attempt to refer to the examples of Facebook and Google.

Question 20

The Ford Motor Company produces a wide range of different vehicles aimed at a range of market segments. Analyse how it benefits from the use of product portfolio analysis.

(9 marks)

ⓔ Remember that 'analyse' questions expect you to show the skills of knowledge, application and analysis. You are not expected to evaluate, so don't waste time making counter-arguments.

Student A

Product portfolio analysis includes concepts such as the product life cycle and the Boston Matrix. It is used by businesses to decide what marketing actions need to be taken for each of their products.

Ford sells a wide range of vehicles, from small cars like the Fiesta to large lorries. Successful products such as the Ford Focus and Mondeo are in the mature phase of the product life cycle. This means that they are producing good profits. According to the Boston Matrix they would be categorised as 'cash cows'. Ford will use the profits generated to support the development of new products. For example, Ford could be developing an electric car, which is in the introduction phase of its product life cycle. Without the profits from the cash cows, the electric car could fail. The Boston Matrix would categorise the electric car as a 'problem child', which has the potential to do well and ultimately become a cash cow. By using product portfolio analysis, Ford can make the correct marketing decisions for each of its products and ensure that it has a balanced product portfolio.

ⓔ **9/9 marks awarded.** This is a good response. It provides a correct definition of product portfolio analysis and identifies a relevant benefit of its use. The benefit is well developed and illustrated using examples of Ford's products.

Student B

Product portfolio analysis is about the product range of a business. It looks at how well each product is doing and where it is in its product life cycle.

Ford will benefit from product portfolio analysis because it can see which cars are selling well and spend more money advertising them. Also it can see which products are in the decline stage and get rid of them. Ford can also use the Boston Matrix to find out which products are cash cows, stars, problem children and dogs.

ⓔ 3/9 **marks awarded.** This answer shows understanding of product portfolio analysis by identifying the product life cycle and the Boston Matrix. It also identifies a valid benefit but fails to explain it in enough detail. There is limited use of Ford's products to illustrate the benefit.

Section C: Essay questions

You will have a choice of two questions. You should write your answer in continuous prose and use examples to illustrate your answer.

A good essay structure is essential. Aim to write an introduction, then two paragraphs that agree with the point in the question, followed by two paragraphs that disagree. Each paragraph should contain a separate argument that is well developed and uses business examples to illustrate the argument. Complete your essay by writing a conclusion that directly answers the question and is supported by your previous arguments.

Question 21

To what extent do you think a leader can guarantee good business performance?   (25 marks)

ⓔ Essay questions require you to show the skills of knowledge, application, analysis and evaluation. It is important that you spend time writing an essay plan before you start writing.

Effective leadership is a critical factor in achieving good business performance. Good leaders have vision, set aims and objectives, give direction and inspire staff. Successful business leaders can become household names and feature regularly in the news. No leader can guarantee good business performance, however. A leader cannot do everything and they are dependent on the efforts of employees to carry out the business strategy successfully. Furthermore, no matter how good a leader, changes in the external environment can have a significant effect on business performance.

Good leaders are able to set a clear vision for the business. They will spot opportunities and devise effective strategies to exploit them. An example of how a leader can produce good business performance is Michael O'Leary, the boss of Ryanair. He spotted the opportunity for budget airline travel in Europe after a visit to the USA. O'Leary successfully copied the business model of a low-cost US airline and used it for Ryanair. His cost minimisation strategy enabled Ryanair to charge significantly lower prices than established bigger airlines such as British Airways and KLM. As a result, Ryanair's low prices attracted large numbers of customers and the business became the market leader. In this case the impressive business performance can be directly linked to Michael O'Leary's vision and strategy.

Effective leaders can also inspire employees to work hard to achieve the business's objectives. Good leaders motivate staff by providing fair pay and conditions, training and empowerment. Mark Zuckerberg is considered to be a successful leader because employees at Facebook are well treated and given the freedom to make their own decisions. Having a motivated staff leads to improved business performance due to higher productivity, lower labour turnover and better customer service. Zuckerberg's management style has been a significant influence on Facebook's impressive performance.

It is wrong, however, to say that a leader can guarantee good business performance. No matter how good the leader, changes in the external environment can affect the success of any business. For example, few commentators predicted the banking financial crash in 2008. As a result, many businesses suffered as banks restricted lending, leading to a fall in investment and consumer confidence. In this situation business performance was directly affected by economic recession; business leaders could do little about this apart from developing strategies to help their business survive.

Another reason why business leaders cannot guarantee good business performance is because ultimately success is dependent on the skill and efforts of the employees. Business leaders can set a vision and devise strategy, but the successful implementation of the strategy has to be undertaken by the employees. Good leaders can motivate staff but this does not guarantee success. Even the most successful business leaders have experienced failure. For example, Alan Sugar's initial success was with his Amstrad computer business, but ultimately this failed when it was defeated by more powerful rivals, despite the best efforts of its employees.

In conclusion, it is wrong to say that a leader can guarantee good business performance. Although there are many examples of successful leaders such as Michael O'Leary and Mark Zuckerberg – who have vision, provide direction, devise strategy and motivate staff – good business performance is dependent on a wide range of factors, most of which are beyond the control of the leader.

(e) 20/25 marks awarded. This is a good essay. It is well structured with an introduction, separate paragraphs for each argument and a conclusion that directly answers the question. The essay is balanced, with arguments both for and against. Each argument is well explained and illustrated with relevant arguments. Some arguments could have been developed further, but overall the analysis would be considered good.

Student B

In this essay I will provide arguments which agree that a leader can guarantee good business performance.

A leader is someone who is in charge of a business and makes all the key decisions. Richard Branson is an example of a good leader. He runs successful businesses such as Virgin Trains and the Virgin airlines. Branson is a good leader because he can spot good business opportunities. He also motivates his employees with his relaxed management style. This means that they work hard to make the business do well.

Steve Jobs was also a successful business leader. He was responsible for making Apple one of the biggest businesses in the world because of products like the iPhone and iPad. Steve Jobs spotted the opportunity for smartphones and was able to launch the iPhone on the market before competitors like Nokia and Samsung.

Another successful leader is James Dyson. He is the inventor of Dyson vacuum cleaners, which had a revolutionary suction system. This gave the product a USP and made it the market leader. Without James Dyson's ideas, the business would never have been successful.

In conclusion I agree that a business leader can guarantee success. The examples of Branson, Jobs and Dyson prove this. Other factors may also affect business performance, however, such as the economy and changes in consumer tastes.

(e) 8/25 marks awarded. This is a disappointing essay. Its introduction is too brief and overall the essay lacks balance. Valid points are made regarding how leaders can contribute to good business performance, with the use of relevant examples. Unfortunately these arguments are not well explained and the examples need more detail. No counter-arguments are made apart from being mentioned in the conclusion.

Question 22

Many markets are dominated by a few large companies. Examples include industries such as aircraft manufacture, soft drinks and smartphones.

To what extent do you think a new business entering a market dominated by a few large businesses would be able to succeed?

(25 marks)

Student A

A market dominated by a few large businesses is known as an oligopoly. Because of the large size of these businesses, it can be very difficult for a new business to compete with them. If a new business can differentiate itself from its bigger rivals, however, it may be able to succeed. In this essay I will discuss the reasons why it is difficult for a new business to succeed against bigger competitors, and will also discuss the different methods it can adopt in order to gain sales and market share.

One reason why it is difficult to compete against larger businesses is that they have bigger budgets for research and development. Aircraft manufacturers such as Boeing and Airbus can spend huge amounts of money developing technologically sophisticated planes like the Dreamliner and Airbus. This is a significant barrier to entry for a newer business, which would not be able to develop planes that could compete with such established rivals.

Another reason is that larger businesses benefit from economies of scale. Coca-Cola can produce millions of drinks each day. It benefits from purchasing economies of scale, as it can negotiate large discounts from its suppliers, as well as technical economies resulting from the use of sophisticated manufacturing. These economies of scale mean that Coca-Cola has low unit costs. A new business may struggle to achieve the same economies of scale, resulting in higher unit costs. As a result it may have to charge higher prices than Coca-Cola or accept lower profit margins.

A new business may be more flexible than a larger rival, however, and be able to respond more quickly to change. A good example is in the UK supermarket sector. Due to the last recession, many consumers have become more concerned about low prices when choosing a supermarket. Budget supermarkets, such as Aldi and Lidl, realised this and attracted customers with their low prices and good quality. Bigger supermarkets like Tesco and Morrisons were slower to respond and as a result lost market share to the budget supermarkets.

A new competitor can also succeed by offering something different from bigger competitors. This is because they are more innovative and can launch new products quicker. This is particularly true in technology industries such as computer games. Due to technological developments, it is relatively easy for a smaller business to quickly develop and distribute a new app or software.

In conclusion, oligopoly markets often make it very difficult for a new business to succeed. This is particularly true when the bigger companies are well established and have high brand loyalty. A new business will usually lack the resources to compete, particularly in terms of research and development and economies of scale. If a new business can spot a gap in the market and exploit it quickly, however, then it can succeed, as shown by supermarkets such as Aldi and Lidl.

ⓔ **20/25 marks awarded.** This is a very good essay. It reveals excellent understanding and contains a range of valid points both for and against. Each point is well analysed and illustrated with business examples. The conclusion is supported and focused on the question, but is mainly a summary of previous arguments.

Student B

Certain industries are dominated by a few large businesses. For example, the soft drinks market is dominated by Coca-Cola and Pepsi. It would be difficult to succeed against these big companies because they are well established with well known names.

One way a new drinks business could succeed is by having different flavours, which would give it a unique selling point. It could also target its drinks to a niche market, such as sportspeople. The business would also need a large marketing budget to establish the product and make consumers aware. The product would need to be really special, however, because bigger companies are able to spend more on marketing their products.

Another way a new business could succeed against bigger competitors is by offering lower prices. If the business is more efficient it will have lower costs. This would mean that it can undercut its rivals and attract customers with its lower prices. Bigger companies, however, may have more efficient ways of making their products, such as better machinery.

In conclusion it is highly unlikely that a new business would succeed, especially if the market it is entering is dominated by a few large businesses. Success would be dependent on the product the new business is selling and if it can offer it cheaper.

ⓔ **9/25 marks awarded.** This answer shows knowledge by making relevant points. It also gains application marks by making some reference to the soft drinks market. Analysis of each argument is limited, however, and the essay lacks balance. The conclusion is based on the previous arguments but is too brief.

Section D: Essay questions

You will have a choice of two questions. You should write your answer in continuous prose and use examples to illustrate your answer.

Question 23

Many businesses, such as Google and Toyota, have been successful because of their culture of innovation.

To what extent do you think an innovation culture is essential for business success? (25 marks)

A business that has a culture of innovation is one in which employees are encouraged to think of new ideas for products or processes. The culture of a business can be described as 'the way we do things around here'. It is the unwritten rules that determine how employees are expected to behave within the organisation. There are many examples of businesses that have been successful due to their culture of innovation, and their leaders claim that it is essential for success. There are also examples of other successful businesses that would not claim to have a culture of innovation, however, but instead consider their success to be due to a number of other factors.

One reason why a culture of innovation is essential for business success is that it can be a way to gain competitive advantage. Google is the dominant internet search engine because it offers its customers innovative products and services such as Gmail and Google Maps. These products were designed by Google's employees, who are encouraged to think creatively. Google has a culture of intrapreneurship, which encourages its employees to think like entrepreneurs and identify new business opportunities. The benefit to Google of this approach is firstly that employees are more motivated because they are given the freedom and independence to make their own decisions. Employees also work in teams, enabling them to share ideas and meet their social needs. This approach links directly with Maslow's hierarchy as Google's employees are able to satisfy their social and self-esteem needs because of Google's innovative culture. As well as benefiting from a motivated workforce, Google's creative employees are constantly developing products that give the business a USP. This enables Google to maintain its dominant position in the search engine market. In fast-moving technological markets, the need for innovation is crucial in order to stay ahead of the competition, so this is a reason why a culture of innovation is essential for business success.

Toyota, the world's leading car maker, is another business that has a culture of innovation. It employs lean production techniques such as kaizen. Kaizen means 'continuous improvement'. Workers at Toyota's factories are expected to have regular meetings to consider how they can make improvements in their work areas. The workers are then allowed by managers to implement their ideas. This is a good example of process innovation, because the workers have first-hand knowledge of how to improve the production process. As a result, Toyota may be able to manufacture its vehicles more efficiently than its rivals. Also, Toyota employs a system of Total Quality Management (TQM), which requires all employees to take responsibility for quality and think of ideas to improve it. As a result of Toyota's innovation culture, the business has consistently produced high quality vehicles more efficiently than its rivals. This provides the business with a competitive advantage, because Toyota has developed a good reputation and has strong customer brand loyalty. This success would not have been achieved without Toyota's culture of innovation.

Other businesses are successful despite the fact that they do not have an innovation culture, however. For example, the leading retailer John Lewis is successful because of the good quality products it sells and the high level of customer service it provides. John Lewis's employees are well trained and motivated by the company's pay and conditions. These include a generous annual bonus based on the profit share scheme. As a result, the employees directly benefit from the company's success and therefore have an incentive to provide high levels of customer service. This differentiates John Lewis from other retailers and provides the business with an excellent reputation, enabling it to attract and retain customers. In this example, a culture of innovation has not been essential for success.

EasyJet, the budget airline operator, is another example of a business that is successful despite not having a culture of innovation. Its main focus is on cost minimisation, enabling the business to charge low fares to many different destinations. EasyJet is very efficient; it reduces its costs through only selling its tickets online and by flying from cheaper regional airports. Because of its low prices, easyJet attracts many customers, enabling most of its planes to have high levels of capacity utilisation. This means that the fixed costs are spread over more passengers, resulting in lower unit costs and enabling easyJet to charge lower prices but still make a profit. EasyJet does not offer an innovative product, but is successful because it offers lower prices than its rivals.

In conclusion, I would disagree that a culture of innovation is essential for business success. There are many examples of businesses that are successful because they offer a better service or lower prices. It is important to recognise, however, that the importance of an innovation culture is dependent on the type of market that a business operates in. Business in industries such as technology and engineering, which make sophisticated products, are dependent on constant innovation in order to maintain their competitive position.

e **20/25 marks awarded.** This is a very good answer. It reveals good understanding of the concepts of innovation and culture. The answer is well structured and balanced, as it contains arguments both for and against. Each argument is relevant, well developed and illustrated with effective use of business examples. At the end of each argument there is a sentence that focuses on the question. The conclusion directly answers the question and is supported by the previous arguments. It needs to be slightly more detailed, however.

Student B

A culture of innovation is when a business has to come up with new ideas for products. Google and Toyota are successful because they are always developing products that consumers like. A good example of this is Google Maps. These are popular with consumers because they can use them on their smartphones. This gives Google a good reputation and a stronger brand name, meaning that customers are more likely to use Google's other products which will increase its sales and profits.

Toyota is also successful because of its culture of innovation. Toyota was the first company to spot the opportunity to make an environmentally friendly car, the Toyota Prius. This is powered by a battery as well as by petrol. Consumers liked this car because it was good for the environment and cheaper to drive. As a result, the Prius has become a bestseller for Toyota.

Culture is all about how employees are expected to behave in a business. Handy identified different types of culture. These were: 'power', where everything is focused on the leaders of the business; 'role', where behaviour is based on your position in the business; 'task', where everyone is focused on a particular job; and 'person', where employees with similar skills and experience are grouped together.

A culture of innovation is essential for success because if a business does not come up with new ideas it will be left behind by its competitors. A good example is Nokia, which became too complacent and was too slow to develop new smartphones. Because of this it was overtaken by rivals such as Apple and Samsung.

Innovation can be risky, however. Many new products fail and all the money spent on research and development is lost, sometimes costing millions of pounds. In this case some companies prefer to improve existing products rather than risking lots of money developing new ones. Also, success is due to other factors like good advertising and low prices. Primark is successful because it offers low prices and brings out copies of new fashion designs quickly.

In conclusion, I agree that a culture of innovation is essential for business success. If a business does not bring out new products, its customers will be bored and switch to competitors instead. It is important to remember, however, that other factors are also important for success.

e **8/25 marks awarded.** This answer shows understanding of innovation and culture but fails to directly answer the question. It identifies valid benefits of innovation, which are illustrated with relevant examples. These benefits are explained to a limited extent but are not linked to the concept of culture.

The answer contains knowledge of Handy's theory, but this is not used to answer the question. There is also a valid counter-argument regarding the drawbacks of innovation as well as the use of Primark to illustrate that innovation is not essential for success. The arguments are not well developed, however.

The conclusion does answer the question and is partially supported by the previous arguments, but it is too superficial.

Question 24

To what extent do you think that maintaining good cash flow is more important than profitability for all businesses during a period of economic recession? Justify your answer.

(25 marks)

Student A

Profitability measures how much profit a business is making in relation to its sales. It is calculated usually by the operating profit margin. Cash flow is the movement of cash in to and out of a business. Managers of a business must ensure that the business is generating good profits for its shareholders, but also maintain healthy cash flow so that it can pay all its bills. During economic recession, many businesses will have an objective of survival. This means that cash flow is more important in order that the business does not run out of cash and become insolvent. Not all businesses are equally affected by a recession, however, and some may view it as an opportunity to increase profitability.

During an economic recession, many businesses will struggle. This is because there is a decline in consumer spending. Consumers may see a cut in their incomes and/or be more cautious in their spending decisions. Businesses that sell more expensive goods, such as cars and holidays, will often see a fall in sales revenue because the demand for their products is income elastic. As a result cash flow becomes more important than profit, because there is less cash coming in to the business while at the same time the business still has cash outflows such as overheads and suppliers to pay. If cash outflow becomes greater than inflow, the business may run out of cash and be unable to pay its bills. Consequently it may become insolvent and go out of business. In this situation the main objective of the business is survival, which can be achieved in the short term only by maintaining good cash flow rather than by improving profitability.

The car maker Honda is an example of a business where sales fell during the last economic recession. In response, Honda recognised that it needed to reduce its cash outflows in order to survive. The business decided to reduce its production to three days a week. This meant that it reduced cash outflows such as workers' wages, energy and raw materials costs. By implementing this strategy, Honda maintained its cash flow and was able to survive the recession.

Thomas Cook is another business that managed to maintain its cash flow during the recession. The business was losing sales because customers were cutting back on luxuries such as holidays or were booking them with cheaper online competitors such as Expedia. In order to continue in business, Thomas Cook had to reduce its cash outflows. It did this by closing many of its high street stores so that it no longer had to pay overheads such as rent, heating and lighting. Thomas Cook also was able to generate better cash inflows by enabling customers to buy holidays from its website at more competitive prices.

For some businesses, however, profitability is more important than cash flow during an economic recession. This is because the recession may offer an opportunity to increase sales and market share as well as to cut costs. Businesses that sell inferior goods and/or compete on low prices tend to do well in an economic recession. This is because consumers have less money to spend and as a result are interested in low prices.

Budget supermarkets such as Aldi and Lidl improved their profitability during the economic recession. This is because their strategy of cost minimisation has enabled them to offer lower prices than bigger rivals such as Tesco and Sainsbury's. Budget supermarkets are able to reduce their costs because they are very efficient. For example their stores are smaller, which means that they have fewer overheads, and they stock fewer products, resulting in lower storage costs. These cost savings enable Aldi and Lidl to reduce their prices, which makes them attractive to cost conscious consumers. Because the budget supermarkets do not accept credit cards, customers pay either by cash or debit card. This means that Aldi and Lidl do not encounter cash flow problems because they have lots of customers who pay with cash. Because of their success, the budget supermarkets have been able to improve their profitability. These profits have been used by the businesses to invest through expansion by opening more stores. In the long term this could lead to further profitability as the additional stores may enable Aldi and Lidl to attract more customers throughout the UK.

Overall, whether cash flow is more important than profitability during an economic recession depends mainly on the type of business and the products it sells. Businesses that sell positive income elastic goods may suffer from falling cash inflows during a recession and have to focus on maintaining good cash flow in order to survive. In contrast, businesses that sell cheaper 'inferior' goods often view economic recession as an opportunity to increase profitability. In conclusion, all businesses should focus on maintaining cash flow, particularly in an economic recession, in order to ensure their survival. In the long term, however, all businesses should focus on improving profitability to ensure that they can provide good dividends for their owners as well as funds for future investment.

ⓔ **25/25 marks awarded.** This is a very good answer. It reveals good understanding of both profitability and cash flow. The effect of economic recession is also well explained.

The answer contains arguments for both cash flow and profitability. Each of these arguments is well developed and illustrated with business examples. The answer has good structure with separate paragraphs for each argument.

The conclusion directly answers the question and is supported by the previous arguments.

Student B

Profit is revenue minus costs. Cash flow is cash inflow minus cash outflow. An economic recession is when there is a fall in Gross Domestic Product. In this essay I will explain that cash flow is more important than profit during an economic recession.

One reason why cash flow is more important is because during a recession businesses will have reduced sales revenue. This means that there is less money coming in to the business because consumers have less money to spend. With less money coming in, the business may not be able to pay all its costs such as wages, rent and suppliers. As a result the business will run out of cash and fail.

One reason BHS failed was because it had bad cash flow. BHS was seen as unfashionable and customers preferred to go to competitors like Marks & Spencer. Also, BHS had lots of high street stores so had to pay high rents. As a result the business failed because it did had low sales revenue but still had to pay high costs.

Another reason why cash flow is more important than profits during an economic recession is because customers cannot afford to buy luxury goods such as cars and electrical goods. Comet, the electrical retailer, went out of business in the last recession because it ran out of money. Consumers were going to Comet to look at products such as computers and televisions, but then bought them from Amazon because the prices were cheaper. This meant that Comet got into more debt with the bank and had to close because it could no longer pay its bills.

These two examples show that cash flow is more important than profit during an economic recession. If a business does not have enough money to pay all its costs then it will fail. It is only when the recession ends and consumers have more money to spend that businesses can focus on making higher profits rather than cash flow.

e 8/25 marks awarded. This is a disappointing answer. Although it reveals correct definitions of profit and cash flow, it does not reveal an understanding of profitability.

The two arguments are valid, but poorly explained and show confused understanding regarding whether BHS and Comet failed due to poor cash flow or lack of profitability. Also, the link with the effects of economic recession on cash flow and profitability is made only to a certain extent.

The answer lacks balance because it fails to provide a counter-argument. This results in a one-sided conclusion that is only partly supported by the previous arguments.

Paper 2-type data-response questions

Question 1

Read the information below and answer the questions that follow.

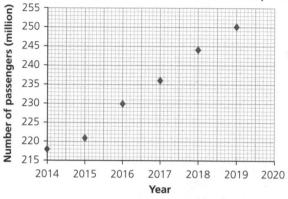

Figure 1 Market size by volume of the UK airline market

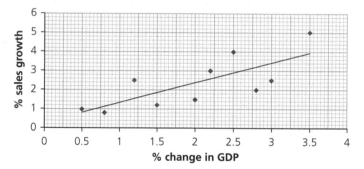

Figure 2 The UK airline market: correlation of sales of airline tickets in relation to changes in GDP

Table 1 Forecasted number of passengers flown per airline, 2016

Airline	Number of passengers (millions)
Bryanair	79.3
Steliosjet	50.5
British Airlines	35.6
Other airlines	64.6

Table 2 Marketing data for the UK airline market

PED	−2
IED	+1.5
Forecast growth in GDP for 2016	3%
Segmentation of market by age	
20–35	30% of all passengers
36–50	50% of all passengers
51–65	10% of all passengers

Table 3 Operations data for the leading UK airlines

	Bryanair	Steliosjet	British Airlines
Capacity (maximum number of passengers that could be flown)	85 million	54 million	50 million
Number of employees	30,000	25,000	20,000
Quality indicators			
Punctuality (%)	75	80	98
Lost baggage (%)	5	3	1
Customer complaints (%)	10	5	2

(a) Describe the correlation of sales of airline tickets in relation to changes in GDP as shown by the data in Figure 2. (3 marks)

ⓔ 'Describe' questions simply require you to offer a brief explanation.

(b) Using the information in Tables 1 and 3, calculate the capacity utilisation for British Airlines in 2016. (3 marks)

ⓔ You are required only to complete the calculation, but remember to show your workings.

(c) Using all the available data, analyse two possible reasons why the owners of Steliosjet would be pleased by its performance. (9 marks)

ⓔ This question requires you to identify two reasons and to develop a line of argument for each. Do not identify more than two reasons as you will not get any extra marks.

(d) Do you think that the UK airline market is an attractive one for a new travel business to enter? Justify your answer. (20 marks)

ⓔ Questions that begin with the words 'Do you think' expect you to show the skill of evaluation. You should consider arguments both for and against whether the UK airline market is attractive for a new business and then weigh one up against the other in a conclusion.

Student A

(a) The correlation is strong and positive. This is because there is a direct link between rising GDP and sales of airline tickets.

ⓔ **3/3 marks awarded.** Correct understanding and explanation given.

Student B

(a) When GDP goes up so do ticket sales.

ⓔ **1/3 marks awarded.** Simple understanding of the link between GDP and ticket sales but no reference to correlation.

Student A

(b) Capacity utilisation = current output/maximum total possible output × 100

Capacity utilisation for British Airlines = 35.6/50 × 100 = 71.2%

ⓔ 3/3 marks awarded. Correct understanding of the formula for capacity utilisation and correct calculation.

Student B

(b) Capacity utilisation = 35.6/50 = 0.712

ⓔ 2/3 marks awarded. Correct calculation but not expressed as a percentage.

Student A

(c) One reason why Steliosjet would be pleased is that it is achieving high levels of capacity utilisation: 50.5/54 × 100 = 93.5%. This means that it is spreading its fixed costs over more passengers (units), resulting in a lower unit cost per passenger. This will enable Steliosjet to either reduce its prices or keep the price the same and gain a higher profit margin.

Another reason is that its customer complaints are at 5%, which is half that of Bryanair. Steliosjet should benefit from a good reputation and use this to attract customers away from Bryanair, which could mean that its market share will rise.

ⓔ 9/9 marks awarded. Two valid reasons, both well explained with effective use of the data.

Student B

(c) One reason is that it has more passengers than British Airlines. This means that it has a bigger market share and will make more sales and profit.

Steliosjet would also be pleased because its lost baggage is only 3% – only British Airlines is better. This will save the business money by not having to pay many compensation claims.

ⓔ 4/9 marks awarded. Two valid reasons identified, but limited analysis and use of the data.

Student A

(d) The UK airline market is an attractive market for a new business because it is growing. In 2014, its market size was 218 million customers. This is forecast to rise to 250 million by 2019, an increase of 14.67%. A growing market indicates that there is the opportunity for a new business to quickly gain sales and market share. Furthermore, GDP is expected to grow by 3% in 2016, the UK airline market has a positive income elasticity of +1.5 and there is a strong positive correlation between GDP and airline ticket sales. This means that there should be increased consumer demand, which a new business could exploit.

The UK airline market, however, is not attractive because it is very competitive. Out of a total market of 230 million customers, the top three airlines are forecast to have 165.4 million customers, a combined market share of 71.9%. This means that they have strong market power and it would be difficult to gain customers from them, particularly as they will have high brand loyalty and large marketing budgets.

In conclusion, the UK airline market is an attractive one because it is large and growing. Although highly competitive, a new travel business could identify a niche in the market, such as business travellers, which it could exploit.

ⓔ 18/20 marks awarded. This is a good answer. It identifies and explains arguments both for and against. Each argument is well developed and there is impressive use of the data to support each argument. The conclusion, although brief, is supported by the prior arguments and answers the question.

Student B

(d) One reason why it is attractive is because the market is getting bigger. In 2014 it was 218 million customers, rising to 250 million in 2019. This means that there is room in the market for a new travel business.

Another reason is that ticket sales go up with GDP. This is predicted to increase by 3% in 2016, meaning that more customers can afford to buy airline tickets. A new business could make increased sales and profits.

Also, 50% of passengers are in the 36–50 age group. This age group has more income than younger or older age groups so will be able to buy more airline tickets. A new travel business could target this age group.

In conclusion, I would say that the market is an attractive one because it is growing and will benefit from more consumers having rising incomes, especially those aged 36 to 50.

ⓔ 8/20 marks awarded. Valid points made, but limited use is made of the data and explanation is mainly superficial. No counter-arguments are provided, resulting in an unbalanced answer. The conclusion simply summarises the previous points.

Question 2

Read the information below and then answer the questions that follow.

ICELAND FOODS has frozen out the competition to be voted the Best Big Company to Work For in the UK by its employees for the second time in three years.

There's always something to look forward to, no matter what level you work at. The annual Christmas incentive, for example, saw people at 51 of its 800-plus stores win a week's wages, while six store managers scooped a 'money can't buy' trip to Ibiza with their partners. Then there's the annual managers' conference being held this year in Dubai (previous destinations have included Florida and Paris) or the retail conference/celebration party for team members and the annual charity week in which all stores participate.

Managers ensure people have the resources they need to do their job, including the basics such as comfortable chairs at the checkouts. Issues such as this are raised by Talking Shop reps, who meet senior managers on a regular basis. Employee engagement is big at Iceland. 'We believe passionately that it is the prime factor in our success,' says inspirational chief executive and founder Malcolm Walker, who set up the Deeside-based multi-billion-pound business 44 years ago with £30 and two freezers. 'We say happy staff make happy customers and happy customers put cash in the till.'

However, in recent years Iceland's sales have struggled. The business has faced difficult challenges such as food price deflation, intense competition and significant changes in consumers' shopping habits. Although the firm has always paid above average rates in the supermarket sector, the introduction of the Living Wage has had a significant effect on its costs. The company employs most of its 24,000 staff in its 859 stores on part-time contracts.

Iceland continues to adopt a growth strategy. Last year it opened 28 new stores in the UK and Ireland. Malcolm Walker believes that it is important that Iceland is constantly looking to innovate the way it does business. 'We have done this by developing a new store format, launching new product ranges, upgrading packaging, rethinking marketing and initiating a major productivity programme.'

Source of information: *Sunday Times*, Best Company to Work For, 2014

(a) Explain how two possible changes in the external environment may have created difficulties for Iceland. (6 marks)

e In this question you should consider two elements of the external environment that are mentioned in the case study and write a brief development of each.

(b) Analyse the possible issues that Iceland could encounter through its strategy of growth. (9 marks)

e You would be well advised to identify only two issues that Iceland could encounter but make sure that each of them is well analysed, rather than identifying several issues with limited explanation.

(c) To what extent do you think happy employees are the biggest contributor to the business performance of Iceland? (16 marks)

e This question requires you to show the skills of knowledge, application, analysis and evaluation. You need to write one paragraph analysing the argument supporting the point made in the question. Follow this with a well-developed alternative reason. Use examples from the case study in both paragraphs. Finally, write a conclusion based on your previous arguments that directly answers the question.

Student A

(a) The article mentions that Iceland has faced the challenges of food price deflation, intense competition and changes in consumer shopping habits. Food price deflation means that food prices are falling. This means customers will expect Iceland to lower its prices. As a result Iceland may have to accept lower profit margins.

Another factor is that Iceland now has to pay the Living Wage. Although the company pays above the average, the Living Wage has still increased its costs. Because of intense competition from budget supermarkets, Iceland may find it difficult to pass on these extra costs through higher prices, as customers will go elsewhere.

e **6/6 marks awarded.** This is a good answer. Relevant factors from the case study are identified and well explained.

Student B

(a) One change in the external environment could be the recession. This means that consumers have less money to spend so Iceland's sales will fall.

Another change is the Living Wage. This has increased Iceland's costs meaning that it will make less profit.

e **3/6 marks awarded.** Relevant elements of the external environment are identified. The recession is not mentioned in the case study, however, so this point would not be given application marks. The explanation for each point is too brief.

Student A

(b) One issue that Iceland could face is the danger of overtrading. Iceland opened 28 new stores the year before the article was written. Each of these would have required significant cash outflows to acquire the store and the fixtures and fittings. If the cash inflow from the new stores is slow, Iceland could encounter cash flow difficulties and be unable to pay its bills. As a result, the business could go into administration.

Another issue is potential diseconomies of scale. Iceland currently has 859 stores. If it continues to grow, this number will increase. As a result it will be more difficult for Malcolm Walker, the chief executive, to measure the performance of each store. Also, problems of communication and co-ordination may result as well as low employee morale. Low morale would be a particular problem for Iceland because one of its strengths is its reputation as a good employer.

e **9/9 marks awarded.** A good answer. It correctly identifies two relevant issues of a growth strategy, each of which is well developed with effective use of the case study.

Student B

(b) One issue would be economies of scale. This is when unit costs fall as the business grows. For example, Iceland could get bigger discounts from its suppliers. If the business gets too big, however, it could suffer from diseconomies of scale, such as low morale because employees lack recognition from senior managers. This could result in higher labour turnover and poor customer service.

e **4/9 marks awarded.** Relevant points are made regarding economies and diseconomies of scale but application marks cannot be awarded because there is no reference to the case study. There is some development of the diseconomy of low employee morale, but not of the purchasing economy of scale argument.

(c) One reason why happy employees are the biggest contributor to Iceland's business performance is that this will lead to a good reputation for the business. Iceland has been voted the Best Big UK Company to Work For. This is because it rewards its employees with financial incentives like a week's wages for the best performers and glamorous holidays. Iceland also provides non-financial rewards such as comfortable checkout chairs and regular meetings with senior management through the Talking Shop reps. Motivational theorists such as Herzberg and Maslow would approve of Iceland's approach. Good relations with management plus comfortable chairs are hygiene factors according to Herzberg, plus the financial rewards as recognition for good work are an important motivator and meet employees' esteem needs. The benefits Iceland gains from this should include lower labour turnover, less absenteeism, high productivity and excellent customer service. As a result Iceland should run efficiently and be popular with customers. As Malcolm Walker says: 'We say happy staff make happy customers and happy customers put cash in the till.'

Business performance, however, is not solely due to motivated staff. In recent years Iceland's sales have struggled due to elements in its external environment. The supermarket sector is very competitive, with large companies such as Tesco and Asda as well as the growth of the budget stores Aldi and Lidl. Despite its motivated staff providing good customer service, Iceland may find it difficult to compete with the marketing campaigns of the big supermarkets and the low prices of budget rivals. Also, as more customers prefer to buy online, good customer service in the stores becomes less important. If Iceland does not offer an online service it may lose market share.

In conclusion happy employees, although important, are not the biggest contributor to business performance. This is because many customers now prefer low prices or the convenience of buying online rather than high levels of customer service. The fact that Iceland is looking to innovate through new store formats, product ranges and marketing shows that having motivated employees is only part of good business performance.

(e) **16/16 marks awarded.** This is a very good answer. It provides arguments both for and against, each of which is well explained with good use of business theory. There is evidence from the case study throughout the answer and it is used to great effect in the conclusion.

(c) Happy staff are the biggest contributor to business performance because employees are a business's greatest asset. Iceland gives its employees rewards like a week's wages and holidays to Ibiza. These rewards will motivate the staff to work harder. As a result the business will make more sales and profits. Motivated staff will also stay longer with the business and take less time off, which will reduce Iceland's costs.

> Happy staff are not the biggest contributor because other factors are also important. For example, if Iceland sells poor quality products it will get a bad reputation and customers will go elsewhere. Also, if its marketing is limited, customers may not know about Iceland.
>
> In conclusion, I would say that happy staff are not the biggest contributor because business performance is about many things.

e **7/16 marks awarded.** Reasonable argument explaining why happy staff are important, with some use of the case study. The analysis lacks links in its chain of argument, however.

Valid counter-arguments are identified but analysis is limited and there is no reference to the case study. The conclusion is too superficial.

Question 3

Read the information below and then answer the questions that follow.

CO-OPERATIVE BANK'S annual pre-tax losses have more than doubled to £610m, up from £264m in 2014. Legal charges increased to £193m, because of higher provisions for the mis-selling of payment protection insurance (PPI). The bank almost collapsed in 2013, after bad property loans contributed to a £1.5bn hole in its finances. Since then, it has taken action to shore up its finances and says it is much 'stronger' than a year ago. It said it had improved its balance sheet and reduced its operating costs through 58 branch closures and staff cuts.

Road to recovery?

The Co-op Bank was the only lender in 2014 to fail the Bank of England's key test of capital strength, which assesses the ability of major UK lenders to withstand another financial crisis. At first sight, the doubling of losses at the Co-op Bank looks like further depressing news for a bank where 'catastrophe' became a routine word.

The discovery of black holes in the accounts, a failure to meet Bank of England stress tests, announcements that were misleading, poor corporate governance and even a drugs scandal are all part of recent history. The continuing pay-outs for PPI mis-selling have not helped its battle to return to profitability.

But riskier parts of the business have now been sold off, customers are not deserting like they were, and the bank's capital base is more solid. Niall Booker, chief executive officer, said: 'Whilst the Bank as a whole will report a loss before tax in 2016 and 2017, we expect a return to operating profitability in the core bank before the end of 2017.'

Its core bank operation saw operating losses of £15m in 2015, down from £79m the previous year. The bank has managed to largely retain its current account holders and at the end of 2015 had around 4.1 million customers.

Christopher Wheeler of Atlantic Equities said: 'The Co-op Bank is in an extremely competitive market. The events of the last few years have tarnished its reputation and put off customers previously attracted by its history and ethical banking policy. It needs to have something else to offer to bring in meaningful returns in the future.'

A group of investors bought a majority share in the bank in 2013, leaving the Co-operative Group with just 20% of it. In 2014, a review of the Co-op Group by former board member Lord Myners said the organisation should adopt a much smaller board of directors and focus on being profitable in order to survive.

(a) Analyse how the Co-operative Bank could use Lewin's force field analysis to manage change in the way it runs its business. (9 marks)

ⓔ 'Analyse' questions expect you to develop a line of argument. It is not necessary to make several points; usually two points (at most) that are well explained and use the case study would be sufficient.

(b) Analyse how a strategy of retrenchment could improve the profitability of the Co-operative Bank. (9 marks)

ⓔ In this question you would be expected to show good understanding of retrenchment and to explain fully at most two ways that it could improve the Co-operative Bank's profitability. Each argument should be illustrated with examples from the case study.

(c) Do you think that changes in the external environment have been the main cause of the Co-operative Bank's poor business performance? Justify your view. (16 marks)

ⓔ The phrase 'Do you think...' is often used in exam questions. It invites you to consider one argument for the proposed reason and one argument against, before making a justified conclusion that definitively states whether you agree or disagree.

Student A

(a) Lewin's force field analysis is a useful technique managers can employ when trying to manage change. Lewin said that the first step was to identify where there is a need for change. In the case of the Co-operative Bank, this could be the mis-selling of PPI. The next stage would be to identify all the reasons for the change and all the factors against it. For example, a reason for the need to change the mis-selling of PPI is the financial penalties that the bank will suffer if it continues. A reason against the change could be staff resistance, as perhaps they received bonus payments for each PPI policy sold. Lewin then said that each reason for and against change should be given a score and then an overall total. If the total for change was greater, then it should be implemented. In the case of the need to stop selling PPI, it is obvious that the score for change would be higher because of the severe financial consequences to the Co-op Bank if it doesn't do this.

Another benefit of Lewin's theory is that it identifies which reasons either for or against change are the most important. If there is significant resistance from staff about changing the way PPI is sold, the senior managers could then focus on how to reduce this resistance. For example, they could introduce a different payment system for staff who sell PPI. By doing this, change can be implemented more smoothly.

ⓔ **9/9 marks awarded.** A very good answer that reveals excellent understanding of Lewin's theory. Two separate reasons are identified and well developed with consistent use of the case study.

Student B

(a) Lewin's force field analysis is about managing change. It means looking at reasons for and against change and giving each one a score. The higher score means either change should occur or it shouldn't. It is good because it forces managers to find out all the different reasons and make a better decision. Lewin's theory would be useful for the Co-operative Bank because it has made a loss of £610m and the new owners will be keen for the business to improve quickly.

ⓔ **4/9 marks awarded.** This answer shows some understanding of Lewin's theory. It also identifies a reason why the Co-op Bank needs to change, but it fails to explain how it could use Lewin's theory to manage this change.

Student A

(b) Retrenchment is when a business becomes smaller by reducing the size of its operations. This can include closing factories, offices or shops.

One way retrenchment could improve the Co-operative Bank's profitability is by reducing costs. For example, the bank has closed 58 branches and made staff cuts. Closing branches means that the business will not have to pay costs such as rent as well as overheads like heating, lighting and insurance. If the bank can still maintain its revenue, the cost savings should lead to improved profits or reduction in losses. The Co-operative Bank's losses have fallen from £79m to £15m, so the retrenchment strategy is working.

A second way that retrenchment can improve profitability is by reducing the size of the business's organisational structure. Lord Myners said that the business needed a smaller board of directors. Having fewer directors will make savings on their salaries, and also lead to quicker decision making because there are fewer people involved. The business is in a competitive market and needs to respond quickly to what its competitors, such as Barclays and Santander, are doing. Quicker decision making such as bringing out new bank accounts before the opposition, could attract new customers and increase sales revenue.

ⓔ **9/9 marks awarded.** An excellent answer showing good understanding of retrenchment and two well-developed reasons explaining how it could improve the Co-operative Bank's profitability. Both reasons are supported by relevant examples from the case study.

Student B

(b) Retrenchment is when a business gets smaller. For example, the Co-operative Bank will save money by closing 58 branches. This will reduce costs and improve profits.

The business is also making job cuts. This means that it will save money on wages as well as other costs such as not having to pay holiday and sick pay. This may, however, lead to a fall in morale and a bad reputation for the bank.

@ **4/9 marks awarded.** This answer shows limited understanding of retrenchment. It identifies a valid reason of reducing costs through closing branches and making job cuts. There is some explanation of how job cuts will reduce costs, but it fails to link this to improving profitability. It also identifies a problem with job cuts that the question has not required. This means that time has been wasted by not answering the question.

Student A

(c) The external environment includes elements such as changes in the economy, legislation, competition and consumer tastes.

A reason why changes in the external environment have been the main reason for the Co-operative Bank's poor performance is the economic recession. The article says that bad property loans in 2013 contributed to losses of £1.5bn. In a recession, the housing market often suffers because houses are very income elastic. Consumers cannot afford to buy houses, and businesses are reluctant to invest in factories and offices. As a result the Co-operative Bank would not have sold as many mortgages. Also, in a recession, both consumers and businesses may not be able to pay back their mortgages. This means that many of the Co-op Bank's existing customers may have gone bankrupt, leaving the business with large amounts of unpaid debt. In this case it was the economic recession that was the reason for the Co-op Bank's poor business performance. Perhaps, however, the bank could have been more careful about whom it gave mortgages to.

A reason why it was not the external environment that was the main cause of poor performance is that there was poor corporate governance. The chairman should have been monitoring the actions of the directors more closely and making sure that their strategy was working. For example, there were 'black holes' in the accounts and the bank has been accused of making 'misleading statements'. Good corporate governance would have prevented these mistakes and avoided the financial penalties and bad reputation that resulted. Sometimes, however, it is difficult for the chairman to monitor all the activities of such a large organisation.

In conclusion, I do not think that it was changes in the external environment that were the main cause of poor business performance. Although the economic recession would have affected all the major banks, it appears that only the Co-op Bank failed to develop strategies that reduced its negative effect. This is proved by the fact that the Co-op Bank was the only one that failed the Bank of England's capital strength test.

@ **16/16 marks awarded.** This is a very good answer. It is well structured, with separate paragraphs for each point and the conclusion. Each paragraph contains a valid argument, is well explained and is supported with relevant examples from the case study. Evaluation is evident in each paragraph as well as in the conclusion. The conclusion answers the question by making a definite judgement that is supported by the previous arguments.

Student B

(c) The external environment is also known as PESTLE. This stands for Political, Economic, Social, Technological and Environmental factors.

I think the poor business performance was due to political reasons. The bank had to pay £193m in legal charges for mis-selling payment protection insurance. This was because the government passed legislation to make sure that insurance was sold properly to consumers. If there had been no legislation the Co-op Bank would not have been fined.

I also think it was social factors that caused the poor business performance. The article says that customers were put off because of the bank's tarnished ethical reputation. Customer tastes change quickly and it is difficult to keep up with these changes.

Another reason was technological. More banks now offer accounts that customers can use with their smartphone. The Co-op Bank may have been slower than its competitors in offering these type of accounts.

In conclusion, I think it was changes in the external environment that caused the poor business performance because it is difficult for businesses to predict them.

ℯ 6/16 marks awarded. This answer shows good understanding of the external environment. It identifies three valid reasons, two of which are supported with examples from the case study. There is only limited explanation of each reason, however. This answer fails to identify or explain a counter-argument. This means that it lacks balance and consequently the conclusion is one-sided. Also, the conclusion is too brief and is not supported by the previous arguments.

Paper 3-type compulsory case study question

Lego

Lego is the world's biggest toymaker. It was founded in 1932 by Ole Kirk Christiansen, a master carpenter. When demand for his stepladders and ironing boards collapsed in the Great Depression, Christiansen started making toys. The toys, the first of which was a wooden duck, proved so popular that he switched entirely to making toys using the brand name Lego, derived from the Danish *leg godt*, meaning 'play well'.

The company flourished under the control of Christiansen's son Godtfred, who joined the firm at 12 years old, followed by the grandson, Kjeld Kirk Cristiansen. However, by the late 1990s, the company had lost its way – the result of a misguided attempt to become the world's biggest children's brand with haphazard expansion into dolls, clothes and books. Lego faced a crisis in 2003; its sales were falling by 26% a year and the company had made a loss of £150 million. As a result, Kjeld Kirk Christiansen resigned and was replaced by a new chief executive, Joergen Vig Knudstorp.

Lego's revival

Knudstorp is credited with returning Lego to profitability. The company has increased sales and profits for the last nine consecutive years. In 2015 it made profits of £900 million and sales revenue of £2.5 billion, a 10% increase on 2014. Lego is now the world's most profitable toymaker. This is due to achieving high levels of added value. Each kilogram of the plastic used to make Lego's bricks costs $1 but the bricks are sold for $75 per kilogram.

Knudstorp's strategy is based on constant innovation and the creation of 60–70 new products every year, including Harry Potter, Star Wars and SpongeBob SquarePants ranges. New products account for 60% of total sales each year. These products succeed in the face of competition from iPads and computer games. Knudstorp places great emphasis on innovation: 'We need to constantly become better, or otherwise there will be someone out there who will catch up to us,' he said.

Jane Westgarth, a toy analyst at market research firm Mintel, said Lego's recovery had been fuelled by its investment in quality and design. 'They are doing things that are taking Lego into a slightly different position, from the boxes of bricks where you had to use your imagination to sets you use in specific ways with characters you already know,' she said. 'If it's good quality, people are prepared to pay that little bit extra.' Lego was also benefiting considerably from targeting parents by exploiting their nostalgia for their own childhood – parents including David Beckham, who admitted earlier this month that he builds Lego with his children to stay calm and had just completed the 4,287-piece Tower Bridge kit. 'For a parent aged 30 there's no doubt about it that they would have Lego in their homes. Parents like to introduce their children to things that they loved as children.'

Another key element of Lego's strategy was to focus on its core competences and maintain high levels of efficiency. When Knudstorp became chief executive, he sold off the Lego theme parks and made thousands of job cuts. Many of Lego's products were withdrawn so that the business could concentrate on making bricks. The range of different bricks made was reduced and Lego's designers were expected to use bricks that could be used in every product range. Each Lego design must achieve sales of £106,000 in order to break even.

Internationalisation

Lego is now sold in more than 130 countries and is making a big push into China and Africa. Exports account for more than 99% of sales. In China, sales grew by more than 50% between 2014 and 2015 and the country represents a potential market of 600 million customers. Lego is opening a new factory in China to supply the Asian market.

Knudstorp recognises that Lego's strategy will have to change as it focuses on overseas markets and it needs to become more diverse and international in its approach. To do so the company is diversifying senior management into four global offices in London, Singapore, Shanghai and Connecticut. Lego now has a total workforce of 15,000 spread across the world and its 250 designers come from 35 different countries.

Criticism

Lego has been criticised by gender activist group SPARK, which claims that only 16% of Lego characters are female, decreasing to just 11% if the new female-friendly Lego Friends range is excluded. Furthermore, the company has received bad publicity regarding the way girls are depicted. Lego Friends, a new range of more life-like Lego designed specifically for girls, features a large proportion of female characters in hairdressers, beauty salons and shops and in bikinis at the plastic beach.

Lego's lack of professional female characters hit the headlines again earlier this year when seven-year-old Charlotte Benjamin wrote to the company, pointing out that: 'All the girls did was sit at home, go to the beach, and shop, and they had no jobs, but the boys went on adventures, worked, saved people, and had jobs, even swam with sharks.' Her letter went viral.

Appendix 1

Figure 1 Net profit of the Lego Group from 2009 to 2015 (in million euros) (Source: Lego, © Statista 2016; additional information: Worldwide Lego)

Appendix 2

Table 1 Market size and market shares of the toy market by region

Region	Market size by value ($m)	Lego's market share	Mattel's market share
Asia	750	3%	3%
USA	450	8%	23%
Europe	650	20%	15%

Appendix 3

Table 2 Forecast GDP growth rates by region, 2017 to 2020

Region	GDP growth rate
Asia	5.3%
USA	2.0%
Europe	0.5%

Question 1

Analyse the importance of innovation for Lego's future success. (12 marks)

e 'Analyse' questions require you to develop a line of argument. Remember to read the question carefully. For example, this question asks you to assess the importance of innovation for Lego's *future* success, so make sure that your answer consistently refers to this.

Student A

Innovation is the commercial success of new products or processes. It is important for Lego's future success, because it is the key to the company's profitability.

Lego makes 60 to 70 new products each year and these contribute 60% of total sales. The business has increased its sales and profits for nine consecutive years and if this trend is to continue, Lego needs constantly to develop new products. New products provide Lego with a USP, because customers will always be looking for something different. Lego has to compete with technological products such as iPads and computer games, so it is essential that it keeps one step ahead of the competition. To quote the chief executive Joergen Vig Knudstorp: 'We need to constantly become better, or otherwise there will be someone out there who will catch up to us.'

Innovation helps Lego to add value because customers are prepared to pay higher prices for well designed, quality products. For example, one kilogram of plastic bricks costs Lego $1 to make but is sold for $75. This contributes to Lego's impressive profits of £900 million in 2015. These profits can then be reinvested into developing new products, which are essential for Lego's future success.

ⓔ **12/12 marks awarded**. This is an excellent answer. It shows good understanding of innovation and identifies two reasons why it is important for Lego's future success. Each reason is well explained and illustrated with consistent use of the case study.

Student B

Innovation is the development of new products. It is important for the success of Lego because its strategy is based on constant innovation and the creation of 60 to 70 new products every year, including Harry Potter, Star Wars and SpongeBob SquarePants ranges. New products account for 60% of total sales each year. These products succeed in the face of competition from iPads and computer games. Knudstorp places great emphasis on innovation: 'We need to constantly become better, or otherwise there will be someone out there who will catch up to us.'

If Lego did not bring out new products it would lose sales because customers would get bored and buy other toys instead. This shows why innovation is important for Lego's future success.

ⓔ **6/12 marks awarded.** This answer provides an incomplete definition of innovation, because it fails to mention that new products need to be commercially successful as well. It contains a relevant reason, but this is simply copied from the case study and fails to explain why innovation is important for future success.

Question 2

Do you think that Lego's use of market segmentation, through developing products aimed at girls, has been successful?

(16 marks)

ⓔ 'Do you think...' is a phrase that invites you to show the skill of evaluation. Remember to write a conclusion that makes a supported judgement and directly answers the question. Do not simply summarise your previous arguments.

Student A

Market segmentation is dividing a market of potential customers into groups that have similar characteristics. Lego has used market segmentation through its development of the Lego Friends range, which is aimed at young girls.

Market segmentation is useful because it enables Lego to target new markets, in this case young girls. This provides Lego with an opportunity to increase its sales. There is also an opportunity to achieve economies of scale because Lego's designers are expected to use bricks that can be used in every product range. As a result, the popularity of Lego Friends means that more bricks are produced that can be used in all of Lego's products. By targeting new markets, Lego has increased its sales, and achieved economies of scale and higher levels of capacity utilisation. The combination of increased sales revenue and lower unit costs led to Lego achieving record profits of £900 million in 2015.

Lego's use of market segmentation by developing products aimed at girls has generated bad publicity for the company, however. Lego has been criticised by gender activist group SPARK, because only 16% of its characters are female. Furthermore, the female characters in Lego Friends feature a large proportion in hairdressers, beauty salons and shops and wearing bikinis. This bad publicity could damage Lego's reputation and the company may lose customers, particularly parents, who may disagree with the stereotyping of the female characters. This shows that the use of market segmentation has not been successful, because it assumes that all groups have the same tastes and characteristics.

In conclusion, it can be said that despite the bad publicity, Lego's use of market segmentation through developing products aimed specifically at girls has been successful. This is because Lego Friends has proven to be a popular product and has contributed to Lego's impressive profits. It is important, however, that Lego responds to the criticism over how it depicts the female characters in Lego Friends and portrays them in more professional roles.

ⓔ **16/16 marks awarded.** This is a well-structured answer. It contains well-developed arguments both agreeing and disagreeing that market segmentation has been used successfully. Each argument is illustrated with effective use of the case study. The conclusion is supported by the previous analysis and directly answers the question.

Market segmentation has been successful because the product aimed at girls, Lego Friends, has enabled Lego to increase sales and profits. This is because girls prefer to buy products with characters they like, rather than Star Wars or SpongeBob SquarePants, which appeal more to boys.

Market segmentation has not been successful because girls may prefer other toys like Barbie dolls. They may not be interested in using bricks to make things. This means that Lego Friends will not sell well and will lose money.

In conclusion, Lego's use of market segmentation has been unsuccessful because girls tend to prefer playing with dolls rather than bricks.

e **4/16 marks awarded.** This answer fails to explain the concept of market segmentation. Instead it simply discusses the arguments for and against selling products aimed at girls. Each argument is explained to only a limited extent and there is little use of the case study. The conclusion is based on personal opinion rather than evidence from the case study.

Question 3

Lego is adopting a strategy of internationalisation by targeting Asia for future sales growth. To what extent do you agree with this strategy? Justify your view. (20 marks)

e It is a good idea to spend time planning your answer to questions that are worth a significant number of marks. In the exam, sufficient time is given to enable you to read the case study thoroughly and identify relevant arguments.

Student A

A strategy of internationalisation is when a business both sells and manufactures its products in more than one country. Lego is targeting Asia for its future sales growth. This strategy can provide Lego with increased rewards but also brings extra risks.

One reason I agree with this strategy is the huge potential sales that can be achieved from Asia. This region has a market size by value of $750 million and currently Lego only has a 3% market share. If Lego could increase its market share to 10%, this would represent $75 million sales. Furthermore, Asia's GDP is expected to grow by 5.3% between 2017 and 2020, which means that the market size will become even bigger. This growth is significantly higher than in Lego's main markets in the USA (2%) and Europe (0.5%). These figures prove that the Asian market has the greatest potential.

Lego is already established in China, Asia's biggest individual market with 600 million potential customers. Sales there grew by more than 50% between 2014 and 2015 and Lego has built a factory in China specifically to supply this market. This should reduce production and transport costs, as well as enabling Lego to supply its products to customers more quickly.

A strategy of internationalisation brings additional risks, however. Ansoff's Matrix would classify this strategy as market development. The risk is that Asia represents an unknown market and Lego needs to be aware of competition from other toy companies like Mattel, which may also be targeting Asia, as well as domestic rivals. Consumer tastes in Asia may be different due to culture and language. This means that Lego will need to spend large amounts of money on market research and product development. Joergen Vig Knudstorp has recognised that Lego 'needs to become more diverse and international in its approach'. There is no guarantee that all the extra costs required to target the Asian market will bring success.

In conclusion, I do agree with Lego's strategy of internationalisation by targeting Asia for future sales growth. This market has the greatest potential as it has a huge market size and is growing. The rise in GDP indicates that more people in this region will be able to afford Lego's products. The company already sells its products in 130 countries and 99% of its sales are from exports, proving that it has worldwide appeal. As long as Lego conducts sufficient market research and develops products that appeal to the Asian market, I am confident that it will succeed.

@ **20/20 marks awarded.** This is a very good answer. It shows good understanding of an internationalisation strategy. Arguments both for and against this strategy are identified and well developed in separate paragraphs. This gives the answer a balanced structure. There is consistent use of the case study throughout to support each argument. The conclusion directly answers the question and is based on the previous arguments.

Student B

Internationalisation is when a business sells its products in different countries. Lego sells its products in 130 countries and 99% of its sales are exports. This shows that it already knows how to sell its products in different countries.

I think it is a good idea that it targets Asia, particularly China, which has a population of 600 million customers. This means that if it can increase its sales in Asia, Lego will make more profit. Also the economy in Asia is growing faster because GDP is 5.3%, compared with 2% in the USA and 0.5% in Europe. This shows that consumers in Asia will be able to spend more on luxury products like Lego toys.

I think it is a bad idea to target Asia because Lego only has a 3% market share of the Asian market. Lego is not very well known in Asia and will have to spend lots of money on advertising. Customers in Asia may prefer to buy products from Asian businesses instead, which control more than 90% of the Asian market. This means that Lego will find it difficult to gain extra sales.

In evaluation, I do not agree with Lego's strategy of internationalisation because the risks are greater than the rewards. It should instead just concentrate on Europe because it is safer and it already has a market share of 20%.

ⓔ **8/20 marks awarded**. This answer is disappointing. It provides an incomplete definition of an internationalisation strategy. Valid reasons both for and against the strategy are identified and illustrated with examples from the case study, but analysis is limited. The conclusion is too brief and largely unsupported. It also includes an additional point, which should have been used earlier in the answer.

Knowledge check answers

1 Increased sales and market share. Reduced unit costs through economies of scale and high capacity utilisation.

2 To reduce costs plus focus on 'core' activities.

3 A takeover may be from a competitor in an attempt to increase market share. A merger may be more co-operative and for the mutual benefit of both businesses.

4 Increased profit margin.

5 Fixed wage costs are spread over fewer units.

6 Diversification and cost synergies.

7 To reduce costs of expansion, plus franchisee is motivated for the franchise to succeed.

8 Entering a new market plus lack of knowledge and expertise.

9 First mover advantage.

10 Maslow (esteem needs) plus Herzberg (motivators of recognition and achievement).

11 Social media, websites and apps.

12 Different language, culture and legislation.

13 Quicker distribution, lower transport costs, more control over quality.

14 Different colours, basic facilities to enable affordable price, smaller engines.

15 Targeted offers, knowledge of buying habits, development of customer profile.

16 Personal service, plus customers can try on the clothes.

17 10:7 in favour of change.

18 Convenience of streaming, wider availability, bigger potential market.

19 Agreed number of total hours worked each year, but employees are expected to work longer hours during busy periods and fewer hours during quieter times.

20 Facilitation and support.

21 Task.

22 Low score for power distance, high for individualism, average for uncertainty avoidance and high for femininity.

23 Employees understand the need for change; set clear vision; appoint right managers to execute strategy; persistence to overcome problems.

24 Advantage: Employees with similar skills work together.
Disadvantage: Departments may work in isolation.

25 70 (14 + 28 + 21 + 7).

26 B, D, F and I.

27 18 – 2 – 14 = 2.

28 Emergent – Google operates in a rapidly changing market.

29 Specific, Measurable, Achievable, Realistic, Time-related.

30 Fire at the warehouse, website crashes, major supplier goes out of business.

Index

Index

Index